Scott E. Donaldson, Chris K. Williams, and Stan

Understanding Security Issues

Scott E. Donaldson,
Chris K. Williams, and
Stanley G. Siegel

Understanding Security Issues

—

DE
G
PRESS

ISBN 978-1-5015-1523-1
e-ISBN (PDF) 978-1-5015-0650-5
e-ISBN (EPUB) 978-1-5015-0636-9

Library of Congress Control Number: 2018962044

Bibliographic information published by the Deutsche Nationalbibliothek
The Deutsche Nationalbibliothek lists this publication in the Deutsche
Nationalbibliografie; detailed bibliographic data are available on the Internet at http://
dnb.dnb.de.

Published by Walter de Gruyter Inc., Boston/Berlin
Printing and binding: CPI books GmbH, Leck
Typesetting: MacPS, LLC, Carmel
Cover Image: Can Stock Photo / KrulUA
www.degruyter.com

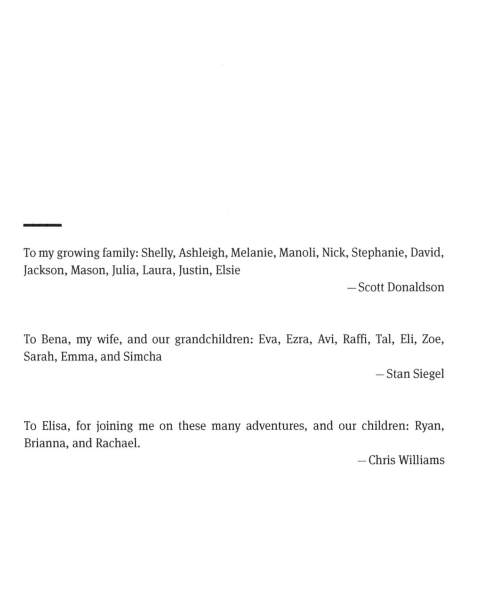

To my growing family: Shelly, Ashleigh, Melanie, Manoli, Nick, Stephanie, David, Jackson, Mason, Julia, Laura, Justin, Elsie

— Scott Donaldson

To Bena, my wife, and our grandchildren: Eva, Ezra, Avi, Raffi, Tal, Eli, Zoe, Sarah, Emma, and Simcha

— Stan Siegel

To Elisa, for joining me on these many adventures, and our children: Ryan, Brianna, and Rachael.

— Chris Williams

About De|G PRESS

Five Stars as a Rule

De|G PRESS, the startup born out of one of the world's most venerable publishers, De Gruyter, promises to bring you an unbiased, valuable, and meticulously edited work on important topics in the fields of business, information technology, computing, engineering, and mathematics. By selecting the finest authors to present, without bias, information necessary for their chosen topic *for professionals*, in the depth you would hope for, we wish to satisfy your needs and earn our five-star ranking.

In keeping with these principles, the books you read from De|G PRESS will be practical, efficient and, if we have done our job right, yield many returns on their price.

We invite businesses to order our books in bulk in print or electronic form as a best solution to meeting the learning needs of your organization, or parts of your organization, in a most cost-effective manner.

There is no better way to learn about a subject in depth than from a book that is efficient, clear, well organized, and information rich. A great book can provide life-changing knowledge. We hope that with De|G PRESS books you will find that to be the case.

DOI 10.1515/9781501506505-203

Acknowledgments

Any book project can not be accomplished without some impact on home life. To our family members, we express our gratitude for their patience while we took a lot of time away from them on evenings and weekends to write this book. Because this time can never be reclaimed, we are forever grateful for their understanding and support.

We thank De|G PRESS, an imprint of De Gruyter, and Jeff Pepper for accepting this project and mentoring us through the authorship process. We thank Jaya Dalal for her careful review of our material at each stage of the process. We thank Denise Pangia for helping us convey our thoughts in clear and unambiguous terms, and correcting us when we went awry. We thank Angie MacAllister and her team for their professional management of this complex and challenging project. We thank Anett Rehner for her thoughtful and detailed review of the final materials before they went to press.

Finally, we thank our reviewers and friends who took time from their busy schedules to review, comment, listen, and advise on our content and ideas. Your inputs made our ideas better than they were before, and for that service we are forever in your debt.

— Scott Donaldson, Chris Williams, Stan Siegel

DOI 10.1515/9781501506505-204

About the Authors

Scott E. Donaldson has professional experience in the defense, federal, commercial, and university marketplaces. His expertise includes multi-hundred-million-dollar program management, systems development, information technology, and business operations and development. He has served in a wide variety of technical leadership roles including, chief technology officer, IT director, and chief systems engineer. He has developed new technologies, techniques, and practices to bring in new business by solving real-world problems.

Donaldson teaches graduate courses in systems engineering at the Johns Hopkins University, Whiting School of Engineering. Johns Hopkins honored him in 2009 with an Excellence in Teaching Award. He has a BS in Operations Research from the United States Naval Academy and a MS in Systems Management from the University of Southern California.

Donaldson has co-authored three software engineering books: *Successful Software Development: Making It Happen*, 2nd Edition (Prentice Hall PTR, 2001); *Successful Software Development: Study Guide* (Prentice Hall PTR; 2001); and *Cultivating Successful Software Development: A Practitioner's View* (Prentice Hall PTR, 1997).

Donaldson also co-authored *CTOs at Work* (Apress, 2012); *Enterprise Cybersecurity: How to Build a Successful Cyberdefense Program Against Advanced Threats* (Apress, 2015); and *Enterprise Cybersecurity: Study Guide* (Apress, 2018).

Donaldson has contributed to other software engineering books: *Encyclopedia of Software Engineering: Project Management—Success Factors (Reducing the Likelihood of Software Failures)* (CRC Press, 2010) and the *Handbook of Software Quality Assurance: Software Configuration Management—A Practical Look, 3rd Edition* (Prentice Hall, 1999).

DOI 10.1515/9781501506505-205

Chris K. Williams has been involved in the cybersecurity field since 1994 in a combination of U.S. military and commercial positions. He has been in the cyber-security field for more than 20 years focusing on enterprise cybersecurity strategy, architecture, and compliance. He is a veteran of the US Army, having served five years with the 82nd Airborne Division and 35th Signal Brigade. He has worked on cybersecurity projects with the U.S. Army, Defense Information Systems Agency, Department of State, Defense Intelligence Agency, and numerous other commercial and government organizations. He focuses on designing integrated solutions to protect against modern threats.

Williams co-authored *Enterprise Cybersecurity: How to Build a Successful Cyberdefense Program Against Advanced Threats* (Apress, 2015) and its companion book *Enterprise Cybersecurity: Study Guide* (Apress, 2018). He holds a patent for e-commerce technology, and has published technical papers with the Institute of Electrical and Electronics Engineers (IEEE). He has presented on cybersecurity at RSA, Milcom, the International Information Systems Security Certification Consortium (ISC), the Information Systems Security Association (ISSA), and other forums.

Williams holds a BSE in Computer Science Engineering from Princeton University and a MS in Information Assurance from George Washington University.

Dr. Stanley G. Siegel has progressive professional experience as a systems engineer, mathematician, and computer specialist. He started his career with the U.S. Government in the Department of Commerce and then the Department of Defense. After his government service, he was with Grumman for 15 years and Science Applications International Corporation (SAIC) for over 20 years. He helped SAIC grow to a $11 billion leader in scientific, engineering, and technical solutions with hundreds of millions of dollars in new business.

Siegel earned a nuclear physics doctorate from Rutgers University. While at SAIC, he served as a senior technical advisor and director on a wide spectrum of projects in areas such as software engineering methodology assessment, software requirements analysis, software testing and quality assurance, and technology assessment.

Siegel and Donaldson have jointly taught graduate courses since the mid-1990s. They teach both in-class and online software systems engineering courses at Johns Hopkins University Whiting School of Engineering. Johns Hopkins honored them in 2009 with an Excellence in Teaching Award.

Siegel has co-authored four software engineering books including the seminal software engineering textbook *Software Configuration Management: An Investment in Product Integrity* (Prentice Hall, 1980) and *Successful Software Development: Making It Happen*, 2nd Edition (Prentice Hall PTR, 2001). He has co-authored *Enterprise Cybersecurity: How to Build a Successful Cyberdefense Program Against Advanced Threats* (Apress 2015) that empowers organizations to defend themselves against the threat of modern targeted cyberattacks.

Siegel has contributed to a number of books, including the *Encyclopedia of Software Engineering, Software Project Management Success Factors (Reducing the Likelihood of Software Failures)* (CRC Press, 2010); and the *Handbook of Software Quality Assurance, Software Configuration Management—A Practical Look, 3rd Edition* (Prentice Hall, 1999).

Contents

Introduction

We live in an interesting age. Over the past thirty years, a concept called the "internet" has revolutionized how we work, play, shop, date, and stay in touch. Smartphones now put the world at our fingertips, and smart homes enable us to turn out the lights from a thousand miles away. Thanks to the internet, we are only one click away from our work, our friends, our shopping, and our information, any time of day and anywhere in the world. Over two decades, the internet has disrupted industry after industry, including: movies, telephones, calculators, watches, shopping, travel, recruiting, taxis, banking, medicine, television, newspapers, magazines, books, and many others.

But all this transformation comes with new challenges, and introduces new risks to our safety and our security. Thanks to the internet, "bad guys" can access hundreds, thousands, or millions of victims with a single click. In 2008 the Conficker worm infected over 10 million computers and placed them under the control of a single set of attackers. The BredoLab botnet gained control of over 30 million computers just a couple of years later. In 2017 the NotPetya attack crippled Maersk shipping by destroying almost all of their 50,000 computers. This one attack disrupted more than 20% of the world's international trade, and cost Maersk more than $250 million in damages. In fact, the NotPetya attack was estimated to have destroyed more than 200,000 computers across more than twenty countries around the world, bringing companies and municipalities to their knees, and disrupting day-to-day life for many individuals.

These incidents have real costs that affect all of us as well as our employers. RiskIQ estimates that global online crime in 2018 cost businesses and individuals more than *$1 million dollars a minute*. Barkly estimated that in 2017, ransomware alone cost over *$5 billion*. Breaches of sensitive personal information abound, with millions of social security numbers, credit card numbers, bank accounts, personal identities, and health care data (that are all supposed to be kept secret) falling into the hands of criminals around the world. According to DarkReading, over 5,000 breaches in 2017 resulted in the compromise of almost *8 billion* information records belonging to regular, innocent people like us. Finally, Statista has reported that between 20% and 50% of all the computers worldwide are infected with some type of malicious software, or *malware*. That is almost a billion computers doing work for the bad guys, every minute of every day.

But there is hope. In this increasingly complex and interconnected digital world, security has become a responsibility not just for business leaders or law enforcement, but for each and every one of us every single day. This book is about how to protect you from the dangers of the internet, while still taking advantage of its benefits, at work, at home, and on travel. This book describes the risks to

DOI 10.1515/9781501506505-207

your digital life, how security experts manage these risks, and how you can contribute to that effort by reducing the risk to yourself, your family, your coworkers, and your friends. So, with all of that said, *Let's get started!*

Your Digital Life

Each of us exists at the center of a "digital life" that includes our home, our work, our relationships, our business, and our friends. This connected ecosystem includes computers, tablets, phones, and numerous other devices that connect us to home and work functions that we enjoy every day (as well as some that we may not enjoy). Most of these devices rely upon the internet to work, so they can communicate with computers, users, and servers hundreds or thousands of miles away. An illustration of this digital ecosystem is shown in Figure I.1.

Figure I.1: Your digital life surrounds you with awesome capabilities.

This digital ecosystem includes resources like computers, tablets, phones, devices, networks, and online accounts. We use these resources to access work functions including e-mail, calendar, contacts, collaboration tools, and work documents. We also use these resources to access home functions such as e-mail, personal documents, photos, e-commerce, social media, gaming, movies, and music. Sometimes our devices are dedicated to one function, such as a work computer, but frequently our devices are shared between work and home functions, like when we access our work e-mail from our personal phone or home computer.

For many of the functions that we desire, connectivity to the internet is required. We may get our connectivity to the internet through cellular networks, cable modems, satellite services, public Wi-Fi, or other network connections. To identify ourselves over the internet, we use *digital identities*—most often a user-name and a password—that identify us to distant computers and prove that we are who we say we are.

Cyber defenses that protect our digital lives must include protections that operate at multiple levels to provide comprehensive protection. These protections must include our devices, our networks, our applications, our online accounts, our online identities, and the online entities we trust with our private and personal information. All of these online resources must be constantly protected from compromise or abuse. Unfortunately, in today's highly interconnected digital lives, a failure of protection in one place may end up having disastrous effects everywhere.

About This Book

This book is about protecting your online digital life at work, at home, and on travel. To achieve such protection, this book provides you with cybersecurity information you should know and can apply in your day-to-day life. This book should help you to answer some of the following cybersecurity questions as you use computers and the internet:

- How do I protect my home or work computer from compromise?
- How do I protect my other home connected devices like phones, tablets, and internet of things (IoT) connected devices?
- How do I protect my online accounts and passwords?
- What is wrong with using kiosk computers, or public Wi-Fi connections?
- What happens when I share information between my work and home computers?
- What rules do I need to follow for my work computer, laptop, or work smartphone?
- What happens when I use my work computer to do personal business?
- Why do I need to worry about online privacy?
- What does my cell phone have to do with my online security?
- What do Google, Facebook, or Amazon really know about me?
- What happens when I use my work computer for personal e-mail, Facebook, or LinkedIn?
- How safe is my credit card when it is in my purse or wallet?
- How safe is my connected home with Alexa, Nest, and Zigbee?
- What happens to cybersecurity when the lights go out?

To help you answer these questions and increase your personal cybersecurity awareness, this book contains guidance on the following cybersecurity topics:
- An understanding of today's cyberthreats and the dangers they pose.
- How to understand cyber risk and use good practices to reduce it.
- Common cybersecurity attacks and how cyberattackers may target you.
- Approaches for protecting yourself at work, at home, and on travel.
- Online security resources that can help you reduce your cyber risk.
- Additional security awareness tips for protecting your digital life.

Who Should Read This Book

This book is intended for a general audience. Everyone should be able to read this book and find useful information about how to protect their online activities at work, at home, and on travel. Readers of this book include the following:
- People who are concerned about security their digital worlds, and the devices and accounts contained within them.
- People who want to understand the cyberthreats targeting them at work, at home, and on travel.
- People who want to understand how their devices, networks, and accounts may be compromised by cyberattackers.
- People who want to learn techniques to secure themselves and reduce their cyber risk.
- Leaders who want to reduce the cyber risk for their teams.

Everyone can use the content in this book to help secure their devices, networks, and accounts at work and at home. By improving their security awareness, people can make it more difficult for cyberattacks against them to succeed.

Contents of This Book

This book is primarily concerned with cybersecurity, while also considering supporting topics that may affect cyber safety. The chapters of the book are meant to be read in sequence, as they build upon one another to help you understand *who*, *what*, *where*, *when*, *why*, and *how* of successful cybersecurity. With that said, you can also flip through this book to specific sections to find useful explanations that may help you reduce your cyber risk.

- Chapters
  - o Chapter 1: Security Mindset
  - o Chapter 2: Common Cybersecurity Attacks
  - o Chapter 3: Protecting Your Computer(s)
  - o Chapter 4: Protecting Your Passwords
  - o Chapter 5: Protecting Your Home Network
  - o Chapter 6: Smartphones and Tablets
  - o Chapter 7: Protecting Your Web Browsing
  - o Chapter 8: Protecting Your E-Mail and Phone Calls
  - o Chapter 9: Protecting Your Identity, Privacy, and Family Online
  - o Chapter 10: Protecting Yourself on Travel
  - o Chapter 11: When Things Go Wrong
  - o Chapter 12: Considering Cybersecurity at Work
  - o Chapter 13: Final Thoughts
- Appendices
  The appendices provide greater detail than the chapters and provide additional examples of security concepts described in this book.
  - o Appendix A: Common Online Scams
  - o Appendix B: The Worst Passwords Ever
  - o Appendix C: Online Security Resources
- Glossary
  The Glossary provides an explanation of terms used in this book, *expressed in plain language* for the nontechnical reader.
- Index

Chapter 1
Security Mindset

In this book we are going to introduce you to the things you need to know to better protect your workplace and your home from technology related security attacks (cybersecurity). The best way to start is to understand our enemies. Later in the book we will examine what they may try to do and how we can protect ourselves.

To understand our enemies, we should put ourselves into their minds and understand their motivations, objectives, and techniques. Once we understand the adversary, we should think a little bit about ourselves. Where and when are we vulnerable? How do we make ourselves more vulnerable? What habits do we have that make the attackers' jobs easier? How can we change some of those habits, and improve our security?

This chapter describes these topics by (1) considering the motivations of the hackers who attack us; (2) introducing malware (i.e., malicious software) and techniques that attackers use; (3) defining a "security mindset" that we should use in thinking about how to protect ourselves; and (4) introducing how security professionals think about security. By being security aware, we can understand what it is we do that attackers are looking to exploit.

What Do Hackers Want?

At the end of the day hackers are people, too. They are computer-literate people who are using computers to accomplish some goal they may think is "right," whether that "right" is making money off cybercrime or pursuing an activist cause that is important to them or to do what they know is wrong. Other hackers are security professionals working to support the interests of their country, which may be at odds with the interest of our country. There are lots of motivations out there. The following list characterizes five types of hacker threats that are common on today's internet:

- *Commodity threats* consist of automated cyberattacks that are placed "out there" by hackers that constantly scan the internet looking for vulnerable computers and devices to compromise. These attacks install malware on insecure computers or through malicious websites or e-mails, but without a specific mission or objective.
- *Hacktivists* take control of computers and install malware to accomplish some activist political goal, or to promote a cause. The group "Anonymous"

DOI 10.1515/9781501506505-001

is a good example, drawing attention to causes or issues the group considers to be important.

- *Organized crime* performs hacking to make money. It might make money by selling stolen information or access to computers to other groups, like nation-states or hacktivists. It might also make money by using stolen credit cards or medical records to perform fraudulent transactions that directly make them a profit.
- *Espionage* involves using hacking to further the interests of a corporate competitor or a foreign adversary. Espionage might include stealing corporate trade secrets and customer information or shutting down online services or manufacturing plants.
- *Cyberwar* involves using hacking to support national interests against a foreign country. Cyberwar might include stealing national security information, disabling foreign computers, or attacking infrastructure like the electric power grid.

Of the above techniques, espionage and cyberwar are perhaps the most devastating in their nature, as some nations have no qualms about wiping out hundreds or thousands of computers at their targets. For example, the attacks at Saudi Aramco and Sony Pictures disabled tens of thousands of computers, and were ultimately attributed to nation-state attackers. However, even hacktivism and cybercrime can be devastating, as we have seen through ransomware campaigns that took out entire medical networks or shut down manufacturing plants.

What Is at Stake Here?

Over the past several decades, there have been thousands of breaches encompassing billions of records containing personal information of people worldwide. These records have included names, addresses, phone numbers, social security numbers, credit card accounts, banking accounts, and health care information. How often have we gotten sent replacement credit cards in the mail, because our information had been compromised? Figure 1.1 shows some of the most recent large breaches, based on the numbers of compromised records.

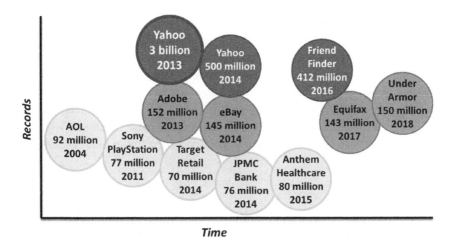

Figure 1.1: Breaches have exposed millions and millions of records.

Some of these breaches involve credit card numbers or banking information and were most likely perpetuated by cybercriminals looking to use that information for fraudulent transactions. Other breaches involved usernames and passwords and may have been performed by hackers looking to use those passwords to access other, more profitable, accounts (since people often reuse passwords for multiple online accounts). Other breaches involved health care information, which tends to be a treasure trove of highly personal data as well as financial details. Finally, some breaches involved potentially embarrassing personal information that could be used to blackmail individuals to get their cooperation. Here are some headlines regarding cyber breaches:

- *Cable News Network (CNN), May 2016:* "… LinkedIn was hacked four years ago … initially seemed to be a theft of 6.5 million passwords … turned out to be 117 million …"
- *Hindustan Times (Major Indian English News Website), July 2017:* "… details of over a million Aadhaar numbers published on Jharkhand govt website … personal details are now freely available."
- *Forbes Magazine, March 2018:* "Equifax's Enormous Data Breach Just Got Even Bigger … brings the total to 147.9 million Americans … driver's license number revealed … social security number exposed …"
- *Fortune Magazine, June 2018:* "… NameTest left the data of 120 million Facebook users exposed online for years …"
- *GBHackers on Security (Cybersecurity Blog), August 2018:* "Firebase Vulnerability Leaks 100 Million Sensitive Records – 2,300 Firebase Databases & 3,000 iOS and Android Apps Affected"

How Has Malware Evolved?

Cyberattackers generally accomplish their goals using malware. Malware is software that is designed to accomplish some nefarious goal, like giving someone remote control of a computer, or extracting usernames, passwords, credit card numbers, or other sensitive information from that computer. Over time, malware has gotten smarter, more sophisticated, and more capable. Figure 1.2 visualizes how malware has evolved over time to gain new capabilities and become more destructive.

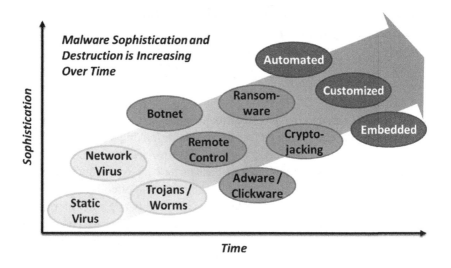

Figure 1.2: Malware evolves to become more sophisticated and destructive.

Some highlights of these different types of malware and their objectives are as follows:
- *Static viruses* embed themselves within computer programs or the computer's boot (startup) process but they require human intervention to propagate, or replicate themselves and spread like a disease, from computer to computer.
- *Network viruses* use the network to propagate from one computer to another and may be able to spread without human intervention.
- *Trojans and worms* are standalone programs that can propagate and persist on their own without requiring a "carrier" like viruses.
- *Botnet malware* reports back to a controller network and enables the victim computer to be used as part of a larger "botnet" consisting of thousands or millions of computers all working together.

- *Remote control malware* permits the attacker to remotely control the victim computer, generally despite network security capabilities like antivirus or firewalls.
- *Adware and clickware* cause the victim computer to display or "click on" advertisements supporting the attacker, generating revenue from advertising fraud.
- *Ransomware* encrypts the files on the victim computer, demanding the victim pay a ransom (typically several hundred dollars) to get back access to their computer and its files.
- *Cryptojacking malware* uses the victim computer to perform "cryptomining" transactions using cryptocurrency (e.g., bitcoin) on behalf of the attacker, indirectly generating revenue for them.
- *Automated malware* can persist and propagate across a network on its own, potentially infecting more and more computers within a target organization, after the first machine is infected.
- *Customized malware* is customized for each victim, or changes itself as it propagates, so it can not be easily caught by antivirus software or traditional network security mechanisms.
- *Embedded malware* installs itself into the "firmware" of network-connected devices or computers, or is already installed from the factory, making the devices almost impossible to "clean up."

Attackers use malware to accomplish their goals of promoting causes, making money, or supporting their nations' interests. Over time, more sophisticated malware capabilities and techniques have become more commonplace, with static viruses being replaced by network viruses and Trojans, and so on. Today, it is not uncommon to run across cheap, network-connected devices that are compromised at the factory, or malware-infected applications in popular mobile app stores.

The Security Mindset

A security mindset is a way of looking at the world "through the eyes of the attackers" to see how they may seek to exploit the world to their advantage. Security attackers are generally smart, capable people whose interests run counter to ours. In short, they want to exploit what we want to protect. Isn't this illegal? Frequently, it is. The problem is that these activities are hard to trace and often cross national boundaries, making legal investigation and prosecution difficult, if not impossible.

To understand the security mindset, we should ask ourselves the following questions:

- What do we possess that is valuable, like our personal information, our financial information, or our company data?
- What potential attackers might be interested in valuable data or capability? Attackers might include hackers, hacktivists, criminals, competitors, or foreign countries.
- How do we make ourselves vulnerable to attack by using our computers to surf the web, open e-mails, or share data with others?
- What can we do to make ourselves more resistant to attack by protecting access to our data, access to our computers, or access to our networks?
- What can we do to detect if we are targeted by an attacker or if an attacker has gained access to our accounts, networks, or computers?
- What can we do to reduce the impact of an attack or enable ourselves to recover in the event an attack against us succeeds?
- If the worst should occur—attackers get ahold of all of our computer data and destroy our access to it as well—how would we clean up the mess and recover?

By considering these questions, we can get inside the mind of the attacker, and think about how things could go wrong and how it might affect us. As the adage goes, "hope for the best but prepare for the worst." When we adopt a security mindset, we think about the things that could go wrong and what we can do to reduce their likelihood, or their impact.

A security mindset involves thinking like an adversary who does not play by the rules and is willing to cheat.

Security Awareness

Building upon the security mindset, security awareness involves thinking about how our activities affect our security posture, every day. We need to understand that actions we take and decisions we make every day can increase or decrease the chance of a successful cyberattack against us, our families, or our companies.

When we are security aware, we are thinking about the security consequences of our actions, and asking ourselves, "Is the benefit action worth the potential cyber risk?" We should apply this question on a continuous basis, thinking about what could potentially go wrong and our preparation to handle that contingency. Some examples of security awareness include the following:

- Keeping personal computing and work computing separate, so the compromise of one won't have consequences for the other.
- Not allowing family members to use your work computer at all, or at least carefully supervising their activities.
- Not opening web links or attachments from people you do not know.
- Understanding that if the FBI thinks you are doing something wrong on your computer, they are not going to let you know via e-mail or a pop-up window.
- Understanding that offers of free money sent to you via e-mail from people you do not know probably are not real.
- Thinking twice about allowing your house guests or friends to use your computers or networks.
- Securing your wireless network, so the neighbors can not use it, however nice or well-intentioned your neighbors may be.
- "Locking down" computers and devices to be used by children, so they can not install their own software or go to "bad" websites.
- Understanding that software licenses, gaming accounts, and game currencies have value to attackers and could be targeted.
- Knowing that when you are traveling, you are vulnerable, and your computers and data are more easily targeted than they are at home.
- Having backups of everything, and multiple backups of your most important data, to guard against all the things that can go wrong.

By adopting a security mindset, and being security aware in everything we do, we can reduce the chances of things going wrong, as well as the consequences when they do. By doing this, we are protecting ourselves, our families, and our company from the cyberattacks that will occur.

Security awareness applies to us when we are at work, at home, and on travel.

How Do Security Professionals Think about Security?

When security professionals talk about security, they tend to speak in terms of *risk*. Is your computer secure? Well, that depends. A computer stored in a lead box stored in a bank vault protected by security guards is probably secure, but it also may not be useful. On the other hand, a computer that is powered up and sitting on your lap at the coffee shop is probably useful but may not be secure. The challenge is to find a balance between these two extremes, where your valuables are protected, while also remaining useful. Security professionals find this balance by conducting a *risk analysis*.

Risk analysis typically involves performing several activities according to a security risk management process. Figure 1.3 depicts a highly simplified process that uses assets, vulnerabilities, and threats to identify *risk*, and then implements *countermeasures* to reduce the risk.[1]

Countermeasures

Figure 1.3: Simplified risk management process.

Assets, vulnerabilities, threats, risk, and countermeasures are defined as follows:

– An *asset* is anything of value to you or an attacker. For example, personal information such as your social security number is an asset, your computer is an asset, and your home is an asset.
– A *vulnerability* is a weakness that an attacker exploits to harm one or more assets you care about. For example, your computer operating system may have a vulnerability due to a missing software patch.
– A *threat* is the way an attacker exploits a vulnerability to cause damage to your assets. For example, a threat is a computer virus infecting your computer due to a missing software patch.
– A *risk* is the potential for damage to an asset. For example, a risk is a compromised computer that an attacker uses to damage one or more of your assets or steal your personal information.
– A *countermeasure* is a security protection designed to reduce vulnerabilities, threats, and risk. For example, antivirus software may reduce the risk of missing software patches by catching malware that has been installed onto your computer.

---

1 Figure 1.3 is adapted from figure appearing in *Analytical Risk Management: A Course Guide for Security Risk Management*, DOD/DCI Joint Security Commission, January 2000.

Chapter 2
Common Cybersecurity Attacks

If we are to use our security awareness to protect ourselves, it helps to understand the objectives of the cyberattackers, and what they might want to accomplish against us personally or against our workplace. What is the value of hacking us? What is the value of hacking our workplace? This chapter considers cybersecurity attacks that may be common at work, at home, or on travel.

To consider those cyberattacks, this chapter describes what the attackers may be trying to do, how they attack, and how we can protect ourselves. This chapter also describes general techniques we can use to reduce the chance of our computers, devices, networks, or accounts being successfully hacked by cyberattackers.

What Are the Cyberattackers Trying to Do?

In general, cyberattacks have three objectives, as shown in Figure 2.1. These objectives are to steal data, modify data, or deny access. Cybersecurity professionals describe these objectives as *confidentiality*, *integrity*, or *availability*.

Figure 2.1: Cyberattacks target confidentiality, integrity, or availability.[1]

A confidentiality attack seeks to *steal data* that is valuable and should be kept confidential. Such data might include account passwords, social security numbers, credit card numbers, bank account information, electronic health

1 Figure adapted from Donaldson, Siegel, Williams, and Aslam. *Enterprise Cybersecurity, Apress, 2015.*

DOI 10.1515/9781501506505-002

records, corporate secrets, or executive correspondence. Attackers may not directly use this confidential information; instead their objective may simply be to collect it and sell it on the "dark web" criminal internet.

An integrity attack seeks to *modify data* to cause disruption or harm. This attack may include changing accounts or passwords, creating fraudulent transactions, or stealing money out of bank accounts. Such attacks can harm an individual's or organization's welfare, self-confidence, financial situation, or reputation.

An availability attack seeks to *deny access* to systems, services, or data by making them unavailable to the people who need them. This attack may include shutting down applications, deleting or encrypting data, or even causing physical harm to devices, computers, or servers. Systems and data that have been disabled by an availability attack may need to be recovered, rebuilt, or replaced.

What Is the Value of Hacking You?

Attackers gain a lot by hacking individuals, and it's more than just your data. When you get hacked, attackers get access to your computer, your accounts, and your passwords. They may also get access to your personal data, as well as your online resources like e-mail, social media, credit cards, or banking. Figure 2.2 shows multiple dimensions of the value that attackers can gain from hacking individuals like you.

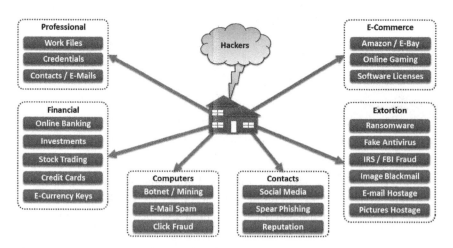

Figure 2.2: Hackers have much to gain by hacking you.

As is shown in Figure 2.2, attackers who compromise your internet-connected computer or device can do many things that may be harmful to you, your family, friends, or workplace. This harm can affect many aspects of your personal life, including your professional, financial, computing, contacts, and ecommerce, as well as direct extortion targeted at you.

Professionally, attackers can gain access to work files and contacts or e-mails that may be stored on your personal devices, or that you may access from the compromised devices. They may also gain access to the credentials you use to access your workplace and may gain the ability to impersonate you and connect to workplace systems without your knowledge.

Financially, attackers may gain access to financial data stored on your personal computer or device, and potentially use that data to steal money from you. This includes access to accounts for online banking, investments, stock trading, credit cards, and e-currency. Attackers can drain your bank accounts, steal your investments, and abuse your credit cards. In some of these cases you may have some protections to limit your liability and losses, but cleaning everything up will likely be painful and time consuming.

Your computer itself is useful. Once compromised, attackers can use your computer or device for their own purposes. Such a compromise can include generating e-mail spam and "click" fraud. For spam, attackers use your computer to generate hundreds or thousands of e-mail messages targeted to millions of users across the internet. For click fraud, attackers make your computer "click on" advertisements of interest to them, generating them revenue from unsuspecting advertisers who pay for what they believe are legitimate customer leads.

Your contacts and connections may be a target. Attackers can access your online contacts and connections, and then use them to target those individuals as well. Attackers can use your social media accounts to get personal information on your friends and contacts. The attackers then send your friends and contacts targeted attack messages they are more likely to trust and open (spear phishing). Finally, the attackers can potentially damage your reputation by making derogatory public posts in your name or by causing harm online to people who trust you.

Your e-commerce can also be targeted. Attackers can access your ecommerce accounts and transactions and use those accounts to generate fraudulent transactions in your name to benefit themselves. These attacks can include e-commerce accounts like Amazon and eBay, but also less tangible online assets like gaming. Modern gaming systems like Fortnite and Roblox include robust in-game currencies that have real dollar value and can be stolen and used for profit. Also, software license keys and upgrade keys can be extracted from your system, and then sold on the black market to unsuspecting users.

Finally, attackers can extort you directly for money or other objectives. These attacks can be particularly unsettling, as they are frequently serious invasions of personal privacy or destruction of important personal data. Such attacks include ransomware, fake antivirus alerts, IRS and FBI fraud, image blackmail, and holding your data hostage. With ransomware, your computer's files are encrypted until you pay a ransom to decrypt them. With fake antivirus alerts, you are tricked into thinking that your computer is infected, and then paying the attacker's "customer support" personnel hundreds of dollars to "fix" your computer. With IRS and FBI fraud, you are tricked into thinking that you have run afoul of the government and forced to pay fake penalties to "clear up" the alleged crime. With image blackmail, the images on your computer or images taken from your webcam camera are used to blackmail you. Finally, with e-mail and picture hostage, your precious personal correspondence or photos are stolen, and you must pay to get them back.

For all these actions, there are markets on the "dark web" criminal internet. Cybercriminals will not only exploit you and your computer but will also sell that exploitation to others in online markets. Once hacked, you are a commodity to be bought and sold in the criminal marketplace!

What Is the Value of Hacking Your Workplace?

As much as attackers can gain by hacking individuals, there is even more to be gained by hacking a company or other organization. When a company is hacked, attackers get access not only to individual computers, accounts, and passwords, but can then extend that access to potentially take control of the entire organization's computing environment. This hacking can include hundreds or even thousands of computers, and gigabytes or terabytes of data. Figure 2.3 shows multiple dimensions of the value that attackers gain from hacking your company or organization.

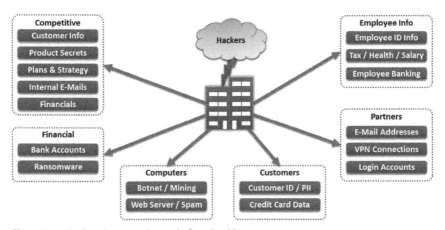

Figure 2.3: Hackers have much to gain from hacking your company.

Attackers who compromise your company or organization can do many things that may be harmful to the company, its business, its employees, its customers, or its business partners. This harm can affect many aspects of the business, including its competitiveness, its finances, its computing capacity, and its ability to protect data belonging to its customers, partners, or employees. Unfortunately, in many cases, hacking a company is not much more difficult than hacking a single individual!

Attackers can gain competitive information against your company. This information can include customer lists and contacts that are useful to the competition, as well as secrets about your products, your plans, or your business strategy. Internal e-mail correspondence may also be useful, or potentially embarrassing were it to be publicly disclosed. Finally, unpublished financial data may be useful to the competition or for making stock trades if the company is publicly traded.

Financially, attackers can steal or extort money from your company. This type of attack can include holding the business ransom by encrypting hundreds or thousands of computers with ransomware, or draining bank accounts through online access to business banking accounts. It is important to understand that businesses do not have the same online protections as consumers, so there may be little recourse against fraudulent credit card or banking transactions. Businesses need to protect themselves from these dangers through other means, like cyber insurance.

The computers at your company can also be used directly by attackers. For example, attackers may use compromised company computers as part of a network (i.e., botnet) used to conduct distributed denial-of-service attacks. They may also use business systems to generate spam messages or to host malicious websites to distribute malware or provide command-and-control functions for other cyberattacks. There is a robust black market in the industry buying and selling access to compromised computers at companies around the world, including many top-tier Fortune 500 and Fortune 1,000 firms.

Information about your customers is also valuable to attackers who have compromised the corporate network. This information can include customer lists and personally identifiable information including names, phone numbers, home addresses, usernames, passwords, and other data. Companies performing consumer commerce may also have databases of credit cards or bank accounts that may be of use to attackers or may be sold to other criminals for profit. Large customer information databases are particularly valuable because criminals take databases from multiple breached companies and cross-reference them to gain even more information about potential victims than would be gained from a single breach on its own.

Being hacked also puts your business partners and service providers at risk. Companies frequently exist within an ecosystem of trust and interconnections between service providers, advisors, partners, and co-marketers. In fact, many breaches occur just to enable professional hackers to get access to trusted partners. They do this type of breach by using direct network connections between companies via account logins and virtual private networking (VPN). They may also use partner e-mail addresses and contacts to directly send attacks to trusted partner users, knowing a message from a known person at a partner organization is much more likely to be opened than one that is anonymous.

Finally, your employees are particularly vulnerable when your company is hacked. Companies possess large amounts of personal information regarding their employees including online identities and passwords, tax information, health care information, salary data, and bank account numbers. Attackers can use this information directly to reroute payroll transactions to their own accounts, stealing employees' salaries, to generate fraudulent transactions directly against employee accounts, or to sell this data to other criminal data aggregators and fraud operators.

To further exploit these attacks, there are markets on the "dark web" criminal internet to buy and sell data and access to hacked companies and organizations. Cybercriminals will not only exploit your company directly but will also sell that exploitation to others. Once hacked, your company is a commodity to be bought and sold in the criminal marketplace!

How Do the Cyberattackers Attack?

Attackers use a variety of techniques to identify, target, penetrate, and exploit their victims. These attacks involve taking advantage of compromised machines as well as human nature to get victims to do their bidding. Frequently, attackers combine two or more techniques together into a single compound attack that is more likely to succeed. Some of the methods attackers may use to penetrate your cyber defenses are as follows:

- **Account hijacking or credential theft.** Attackers attempt to obtain usernames and passwords to your online accounts, and then directly access those accounts by impersonating you. They may get this information from websites that have been breached, or attackers close to you may simply look over your shoulder (shoulder surfing) while you are using your computer, tablet, or phone.

- **Botnet devices.** Home and work networks have exploded with network-connected devices like smart TVs, smart refrigerators, smart thermostats, smart locks, smart speakers, and home assistants. While most of these devices are legitimate and safe, they all run embedded operating systems and may be vulnerable to compromise. Sometimes, these devices are compromised at the factory and arrive in your home already reporting to external botnets or command-and-control. Once compromised, these devices can be exploited by attackers for lateral movement into the rest of your home or work network.

- **Lateral movement.** Once attackers have compromised one computer on a local network, it becomes easier to compromise other devices on that network using lateral movement. Lateral movement involves exploiting network protocols like Windows™ networking or File Transfer Protocol (FTP) that are not generally enabled on the internet but may be accessible once an attacker is inside a private network. Lateral movement may also involve exploiting trust between multiple computers. For example, if you configure your work computer to be able to access files on your home computer, and if one of these computers is compromised, then it is easier for attackers to get to the other connected computers.

- **Malicious applications/adware/spyware.** One of the easiest ways to compromise a user's device or computer is to simply convince the user to install malicious software. Many times, attackers disguise their malware within a "free" tool that is otherwise useful. For example, this tool may be software for downloading movies or getting free music. This malware may include malicious back doors into your system, advertising software (adware), or spying tools (spyware) that send your private data to the attackers or their associates.

- **Malicious websites/malvertising.** Attackers may set up malicious websites and then direct you to those sites from e-mail messages, or you may reach these sites on your own. Malicious sites may also appear to be legitimate sites where you have an account to obtain your online credentials (such as for banking or social media). Attackers may also embed malicious data into legitimate sites that they have compromised, or into online advertisements delivered through legitimate sites (malvertising). Malicious websites attempt to get you to install malicious software (malware), or to exploit a flaw in your web browser or operating system to install malware onto your system.
- **Spam/phishing/spear phishing.** Attackers may send you e-mails, either en mass (spam), or directly to you (phishing/spear phishing). Spear phishing e-mails may appear to come from people you know. These e-mails may contain links to malicious websites, ask you to call fraudulent call centers, or have infected or malicious documents or programs attached to them.
- **Viruses/infected documents.** Similarly, malicious software may be attached to legitimate applications or documents, and be triggered to execute when it is downloaded, opened, or run. The virus then installs itself into the victim's system, often downloading additional components from the internet via malicious websites or command-and-control servers. This approach is a useful technique for propagating malicious software from one user to other people who trust them, via e-mail, web attachments, or other communications.

Once attackers have established this initial exploit, they can exploit this foothold to compromise you, your accounts, your data, and your workplace further. Complex attacks may use multiple exploits and multiple steps to get to the computers and the accounts that are of interest to the attackers. Once the attackers have gotten the access they desire, some common objectives may include:
- **Cryptomining.** Cryptocurrency (e.g., bitcoin) has turned into big business, and requires a large pool of computers be used to support the cryptocurrency business through a process called *cryptomining*. Cryptomining is an energy intensive process (which costs money), so attackers are all too happy to use someone else's computer and energy bill to do it. Attackers may use your computer or your company's computers to do their cryptomining, pocketing the profit while leaving you with the energy bill.
- **Data theft.** Attackers may profit by stealing your data. While more common in commercial environments where there are valuable databases of customer information and credit card numbers, even individual personal data may be valuable. Online statements containing banking account numbers may be used for identity theft, or other personal data may be sold on black market exchanges or used to blackmail the owner. Your data may also be used to

target other individuals, companies, or other organizations for follow-on attack.

- **Identity theft.** One of the most common online objectives is identity theft. Attackers want to steal your identity or your credentials and then use your identity for financial profit. The profit may be getting credit in your name, buying things with your credit cards, directly accessing your bank accounts, or selling your identity to others who aggregate it and sell it to fraudsters. In addition to online approaches, identity theft can be perpetrated the old-fashioned way by obtaining your personal data from discarded papers like preapproved credit card applications.

- **Ransomware.** By far the most destructive of the major attack objectives, ransomware has exploded onto the scene over the past couple of years, only recently losing ground to cryptomining in popularity. With ransomware, the victim's computer files are encrypted using a key that is only known to the attacker. To get the files back, victims must pay a ransom (typically around $500 per computer) to get the key to decrypt the files. Some ransomware, like the NotPetya worm of 2017, does not actually include a key and effectively destroys its victims' files even if they do pay.

- **Spyware and adware.** Once your computer is compromised, attackers may use it to spy actively on you, sending your personal data to criminal data aggregators or presenting you advertisements that benefit the attackers via advertising exchanges. Note that this advertising is legitimate business, except that you did not volunteer to install the advertising software on your computer!

These are only a few of the most common attack techniques and objectives. In addition to the above, professional attack groups target victims with telephone calls, SMS messages, social media, and other channels. Attackers may try to take over one account, and then use "password reset" mechanisms to then gain access to other accounts.

The website www.haveibeenpwned.com tracks millions of identities that have been breached in numerous high-profile attacks. You can enter your e-mail address into the website and see if your account has been compromised. If your account has been compromised, you should probably change your password, if you haven't done so recently.

How Can We Protect Ourselves?

In general, protecting ourselves involves protecting our devices, our software, our networks, and our accounts from compromise. It also involves being vigilant to catch a compromise when it occurs, and to respond quickly to the compromise. Finally, it involves being prepared to respond and recover when something bad happens, with software and data backups, and alternate methods of account access. Some general tips that you can employ include the following:

- **Computer cameras.** Your computer or device camera may be on and recording at any time, even if the activity light is not lit. Malicious software may activate your camera and use it to try to obtain incriminating or embarrassing video that could be used to blackmail you. Cover your camera lens with a physical cover to be sure that it is not being used without your knowledge.

- **Credit cards, ATMs, and transactions.** Modern credit cards include contactless "tap and pay" features that can be exploited by well-equipped fraudsters. Watch out for "skimmers" on credit card terminals or at ATMs that may try to copy your cards or generate fraudulent transactions. Where available, use Europay, Mastercard, and Visa (EMV) chip-based cards that are far more resistant to attack than the old magnetic strips. When keying in your personal identification number (PIN), cover the keypad with your hand to protect against attackers who are watching you or who have set up a camera to capture peoples' entries.

- **Data backups.** If your data is important, back it up. If it is really important, back it up multiple times. Using "cloud" backup services, you can backup your data automatically, but know that some ransomware will attempt to encrypt backups as well, so they may not be entirely safe. For your most important files, make a backup copy periodically—say once a quarter—and store that backup offline in a safety deposit box or something similar. Encrypt your backups but make sure you have or know the key to decrypt them if there is a disaster.

- **E-Mail links and attachments.** E-mail messages are by far the most common avenue attackers use for access to victims and their computers today. Only open e-mail attachments or click on links where you know who the sender is, and you expect the document or the link. Check links to make sure they are what they appear to be—for example, a link from your bank should point to the bank's website and not some other site. Check attachments to make sure they are what they appear to be. Documents should appear to be documents, not programs, and should not request to install anything when they are opened. Be very, very, cautious when installing any software that came from some sort of online message or notification. When in doubt, go directly to the vendor's site or look up the software in the app store instead.

- **Online credentials and emergency access.** Consider the value of your online accounts and protect access to those accounts accordingly. Some accounts may offer multifactor authentication (MFA) for additional protection. Understand the password reset mechanism and how it may be dependent on e-mail or other accounts that might be more easily compromised than the account itself.
- **Password management and emergency access.** Use strong passwords that are not easily guessed and contain a mix of lowercase alpha characters, uppercase alpha characters, numbers, and symbols. Be careful sharing credentials between multiple accounts, as a breach of one account could be used to get access to the other accounts. If you use a password manager, understand the consequences if the password manager is compromised, or if your access to it is lost. Some general password tips are as follows:
  - o   Use passwords that would be hard for someone to guess.
  - o   Do not use the same password for multiple accounts.
  - o   Do not store passwords or password hints in places where casual observers would see them.
  - o   Change passwords regularly and avoid reusing old passwords.
  - o   Consider using password management tools to automatically create and manage complex and/or strong passwords for you.
  - o   Understand your options if your passwords are lost or changed without your authorization.
- **Patching, malware protection, and host firewalls.** Keep your computer, devices, network equipment, and applications up-to-date and fully patched. Watch out for "critical" vulnerabilities in the press that affect web browsers, or tools like Java or Flash that could be exploited to take control of your computers or devices. Where available, turn on "automatic updating" to keep your software patched, automatically. Similarly, install malware protection on your computer, and configure it for automatic updating and to scan removable media. Where available, enable the built-in "host firewall" to ensure your computer can not be contacted by attackers who get access to your network or who are on a public network to which you connect.
- **Personal networks and firewalls.** Protect your personal network with a firewall that separates it from the internet and blocks all traffic except for e-mail, web browsing, and other needed protocols. If you use a Wi-Fi network, make sure it is configured with a strong password and uses the latest secure wireless networking protocols. Do not allow remote access to your personal network unless necessary and then only after it has been con-

figured to require a secure logon. Check your manufacturer's documentation to make sure that your router and modem are up-to-date with the latest firmware (programs to run the hardware) and to patch any vulnerabilities. Be careful leaving personal networking like Bluetooth enabled when it is not in use, as it can be used to attack your devices or your home network.

- **Pop-ups and pop-up advertisements.** Be very wary of "pop-up" messages that appear over websites that you are visiting or that appear on your computer unsolicited. Frequently, these messages are malvertising, or scams intended to dupe unsuspecting users. A popular scam involves encouraging the user to call a "technical support" support line. If you should encounter this scam:
  o Do not call the number that pops up on the screen. If you receive an unsolicited call about your computer, know that it is most likely *also* a scam.
  o Only give remote access to your computer to people whom you know and trust.
  o Never share your password or control of your computer to someone who calls you unsolicited.
  o If a pop-up message appears and will not go away, press Ctrl-Alt-Del (on a PC) to open Task Manager and stop the offending program. You may also need to restart your computer.
  o If the pop-up continues even after restarting, you may need to get technical support to remove the malicious software.
- **Portable media.** Any time you take large amounts of personal data outside your home, it should be protected. Encrypt the hard drives on portable laptop computers and portable media devices like removable drives and "thumb drives" if they are going to contain sensitive data. Put passwords on your laptop computers and smartphones. Enable "remote wipe" capability for your smartphone, so it can be remotely erased if it is lost.
- **Public networks.** Use caution when connecting to unsecured "public" networks like at coffee shops, airports, hotels, or conventions. Others may be able to monitor your network activity, and malicious computers may try to connect to your computer or device to attempt to compromise it. Ensure your personal firewall is enabled, and watch for signs of attack, like unsolicited messages, invitations, pop-ups, or attempts to install software.
- **Smart devices.** Many smart devices send data outside your network to the internet. Televisions or home assistants with "voice control" may be listening to every word you speak and sending that data out to the manufacturer. Embedded cameras may be recording everything they see and sending it out to the internet. You may want to block such transmissions to protect your

privacy. You may also wish to disable automatic content recognition (ACR) features that track your personal viewing activity and share it with manufacturers and advertisers.

- **Smartphones.** Your smartphone is an amazing piece of equipment, but it can also be targeted just like a personal computer. Be cautious about what apps you install, what websites your visit, and what e-mails you open. Be careful with capabilities like Bluetooth networking, built-in cameras, and location tracking, as they can be used to track you and your activities.
- **Social media.** While social media is extremely useful for keeping track of contacts and staying in touch, it is also prone to attack. Do not be the friend who gets all their friends infected with malware and do not fall victim if one of your friends is infected and tries to attack you. *Assume that everything you post online is public and could appear on the front page of your favorite newspaper or news site.* Additional tips for using social media include:
  - o Understand how your social media accounts may interconnect with each other—for example, automatically accessing and uploading your contacts to the social media site or forwarding your "likes" to Twitter.
  - o Look at your privacy settings, and make sure the minimum amount of information is shared publicly, and even with your friends and acquaintances.
  - o Be careful whom you "friend," especially when they are only acquaintances or you do not know them at all. They might be scammers.
  - o Be careful "liking" online content, as you are attaching your online identity to that content. Likes are often publicly accessible and can be used to profile you over time.
  - o Do not post personally identifiable information like your home address, phone numbers, birthdate, place of birth, parents' names, or social security numbers. Watch out for personal information that may be contained in photographs or videos you post.
- **Text messaging.** Attackers may attempt to reach you via text message or may attempt to intercept website multifactor authentication that uses text messaging. Only respond to text messages from senders you know to avoid validating your phone number to potential scammers, who may then follow up by trying to call you for personal information. Do not open links embedded in text messages, unless you know exactly what they are and who sent them.
- **Web browsing.** Use care when "surfing" the web and remember that even major, legitimate websites may be malicious due to malvertising or a temporary cybersecurity incident. Do not search for free versions of commercial software, as they are most likely malicious and hosted by malicious sites. The same advice goes for trying to get free access to copyrighted material like

movies, music, or books. Just like when you go to "the bad part of town," the shadier your intentions are online, most likely the websites you visit will be shady as well. Finally, know that when you visit an insecure website using the "HTTP" protocol, your activity can be monitored by anyone on your network. For best security, use a secure "HTTPS" connection that shows a lock symbol in your browser window.

The remainder of this book discusses your digital life in greater detail, and considers how you can apply these techniques at home, on travel, and in the workplace. This discussion considers protection for your computers, your passwords, your networks, and your mobile devices. It considers how to apply these protections while browsing the web, handling e-mail, and dealing with phone calls. By applying these protection techniques, you can improve the security of your identity, privacy, and family online.

Chapter 3
Protecting Your Computer(s)

For most of us, our computer is the starting point for cyber defense. Whether it is a personal computer, a family computer, or a work computer, modern machines can run hundreds (or thousands) of useful programs, store terabytes of data, and of course connect us to the world of the internet. We use our computers daily to look up information, do our work, connect with friends, create documents, shop for necessities, and manage our money. If our computer is compromised—that is, if our computer is under the control of someone else—all of that is put at risk. An attacker who has compromised our computer can access everything we see or do with our computer, and use that information to cause us professional, personal, financial, or emotional harm.

So, protecting our computer is a key security priority. Fortunately, modern personal computers are tough, resilient, and are designed to be able to resist attack. It is unlikely that something will happen to your computer that will damage the machine itself so that you must get a new one or replace its components. However, personal computers are not indestructible. Just as modern cars are incredibly safe against accidents but can not prevent you from driving them into a tree, modern computers can protect you and your data, but can not prevent you from making mistakes or having accidents that are damaging.

This chapter describes ways you can protect your computer and the important data it contains from possible compromise, abuse, or malicious software.

Securing Your Operating System

The first line of defense for your computer is the operating system. Microsoft Windows, Apple Macintosh MacOS, and the various versions of Linux are the three most common personal computer operating systems. However, these operating systems are hardly the only possibilities. Hundreds of operating systems have been developed over the years, with dozens of versions of each operating system. There are literally thousands of possibilities. However, all operating systems are not created equal. Older operating systems are often highly vulnerable to attack, because they lack protections against modern attacks or contain vulnerabilities that have not been fixed by the developers. Unfortunately, newer operating systems require more storage and faster processors that may not be available on older computer hardware.

DOI 10.1515/9781501506505-003

To secure your operating system, you should do the following:

- **Run a modern operating system.** Modern operating systems, like Windows 10, MacOS 10, or Ubuntu Linux 18, include protections against modern cyber-attacks and are regularly updated with *patches* for vulnerabilities. Operating system vulnerabilities are found regularly, so you need to be on an operating system that is receiving regular patches against known vulnerabilities. If you have an older computer that can not run a current operating system, it is time to upgrade.

- **Patch your operating system.** The most modern, most secure operating system will not last long on the internet if it is not regularly patched. Back in 2004, a researcher connected an unpatched Windows XP machine to the internet and found that it was infected with malware 20 minutes later. Today, it would probably be infected faster. You *must* patch your operating system. Most modern operating systems include auto-update functions that automatically install the latest patches and reboot the computer when you are not using it. Make sure this feature is turned on.

- **Maintain your drivers.** Another component of your operating system's security is the *software drivers* that allow it to support peripherals like graphics cards, cameras, printers, mice, or keyboards. Most of this software is built-in to the operating system or comes from the peripheral manufacturers. Because the software drivers interact directly with the hardware, they can be exploited to compromise a computer's operating system. Make sure you are running current drivers from the manufacturer's website. Watch out for third-party drivers and software that claim that they will update all of your drivers to the current versions—many of these tools are *malware*.

- **Watch out for zero-day vulnerabilities.** Just because you are running a fully-patched and hardened modern operating system does not make you invulnerable. Attacks called *zero-days* will succeed against a fully-patched system, along with attacks that exploit an application vulnerability or trick the user in some way. Your computer can still get infected or compromised, even if you have done everything else correctly.

Securing Your Applications

Your next line of defense centers around the applications you use on your computer. For most of us, the most important application on our computer is the *web browser*, but it is hardly the only application out there. Applications include word processors, spreadsheets, presentation tools, e-mail programs, organizers, financial tools, and of course games. Applications may also include utilities to help maintain your computer or deliver additional functionality like *Java* application support, *Flash* video streaming, or *Adobe Acrobat* document viewing.

To secure your applications, you should do the following:
- **Run current versions of applications.** Applications, like operating systems, become obsolete. Applications that regularly interact with the internet, like web browsers, are highly vulnerable to attack if they are not current and up-to-date. Older applications may be exploited by cyberattackers to compromise your computer. If you need to run an obsolete application, do not use it to connect to the internet, and retire it as soon as possible.
- **Update and patch your applications.** Applications frequently get patches and updates. For some applications like Microsoft Office, application patches may be handled automatically for you. For other applications, you need to periodically go to the application vendor's website to check for updates and patches. Some applications have a built-in "check for updates" function. When an application update is available, make sure you install it and restart your computer afterward, if you are prompted to restart. Your work computer may be set up already to download patches. However, if you are getting messages telling you to update, check with your systems administrator to make sure your patches are working and if there is some action required of you.
- **Remove old or unused applications.** Every application installed on your computer is a potential vulnerability. The more applications you have installed, the greater the chance one of them is malicious or vulnerable and jeopardizes the security of the rest of your computer. Periodically check your computer for applications you do not use any more—remember that tool you installed last year and only used once—go ahead and remove it. If you have a work computer, make sure you check with your systems administrator before removing software that came with your computer.
- **Keep track of your license keys.** While a lot of the software we may install from the internet is free, many of our most important software tools, as well as our favorite games, are purchased and *licensed* to us. Those licenses are usually secured with license keys that may come in the software box or get e-mailed to us if we purchase the software online. Create a file—either physical or virtual—to store your license keys and keep track of them. You do not want to have to repurchase your software just because the original license key got lost.

Using Antimalware Protection and Personal Firewall

Many modern operating systems include "defender" features that help protect our computers from compromise or malicious software. These features may also be referred to as *antivirus*, *antispyware*, or *antimalware* tools. They may also be obtained from third-party security companies like McAfee, Symantec, ESET, and others and are generally available through an annual or monthly subscription payment. These programs usually deliver the following features:

- Secure your computer configuration.
- Recognize known virus, spyware, and malware programs.
- Detect software behavior that may be malicious.
- Increase security for web browsing and e-mail.
- Firewall to filter inbound and outbound connections.
- Protect your passwords, privacy, and payment information.
- Protect your family members using the internet.
- Protect your computer and data against ransomware attack.
- Help backup and restore your computer.

Not all antimalware packages have all of the above features, and some of the more advanced packages may have additional features, but the above features are some typical capabilities to expect. Operating system built-in antimalware protection is usually less capable than third-party products, but it has the advantage of being free, built-in, and usually automatically enabled. While it is usually possible to run multiple protection products simultaneously on a single computer, multiple protection packages may also interfere with each other, if they are all enabled for the same protection capabilities.

When using antimalware protection and a personal firewall, you should consider the following:

- **Install current antimalware protection.** Like with applications, you want to make sure you are running current antimalware software. The five-year-old antimalware software that came with your computer is not going to protect you, if it has not been maintained and updated.
- **Ensure antimalware protection is turned on.** It is easy to have antimalware protection installed, and then to accidentally disable it. Many malicious software programs disable antimalware protection as well. Periodically check your antimalware protection to ensure it is active and operating.
- **Ensure antimalware protection auto-update is enabled.** For antimalware software to be effective, it needs to be updated with current malware software signatures (i.e., identifiers) and the latest attack patterns. Oftentimes,

antimalware software updates come out *daily*, due to the rapid emergence of new threats. If your computer has been turned off for a while, let the antimalware software update before you read e-mail or surf the web to unfamiliar websites.

- **Enable inbound and outbound firewall, if available.** Most personal security products include a firewall as well as antimalware protection. A firewall controls the network traffic in and out of your computer, and limits what programs can communicate with the network. For example, your web browser communicates with the internet, while a word processing program usually does not need such communication to work on locally stored documents. A host firewall also limits the internet's ability to connect to your computer, which may protect your computer even if its operating system has vulnerabilities.
- **Watch out for free "security" products.** Many malicious software packages masquerade as free products to "enhance" your security or otherwise protect your system. If it were free, how would they develop good security? This software is usually malicious, or at least not as effective as it purports to be.

Limiting Administrative Privileges

Another feature of modern operating systems is the ability to limit *systems administration privileges*. What is systems administration? Systems administration is the ability to configure your computer's operating systems and programs. Most of the time when we use our computer, we are just using it, not reconfiguring it. Opening an e-mail or viewing a website should not require re-configuring your computer or installing new software! Limiting systems administration privileges means that most of the time you use the computer in a *nonprivileged role* that is not allowed to change the computer configuration. If you want to change your configuration, you must go through an additional step to escalate your privileges before you can make the configuration change or install software. This systems administration protection guards against programs trying to install themselves without your knowledge. An attempt to change your system configuration triggers the protection and prompts you to check if you really want to allow the configuration change.

To limit administrative privileges, you should do the following:
- **Configure non-administrator accounts.** Modern operating systems can support multiple users of a computer. Most of those users—particularly chil-

dren—do not need administrator privileges and should not be allowed to install software or reconfigure the computer on their own.

– **Use systems administrator protection.** Even if you are the owner of the computer, you do not need to be a system administrator all of the time. On Windows, this is called User Account Control (UAC); on MacOS and Linux it is the "root" user. Administrator accounts should not be used for normal day-to-day use of your computer.

– **Watch out for administrative prompts.** When systems administration protection is enabled, you should be prompted when software tries to install itself or otherwise configure your system. You will see this prompt when you choose to install a program, or make certain configuration changes to your operating system. If you see this prompt when you do not expect it, pay attention! Click "no" or "cancel" and look at whatever you were doing. If you were at a website or opening an e-mail or document, most likely that website, e-mail, or attachment is malicious. Stop and do not proceed!

Controlling Your PC Camera

Modern computers and mobile devices have cameras, just like smartphones. These cameras are usually used to enable video conferencing and are located above the screen on laptop computers. On desktop computers, they may be built in to your monitor, or a separate peripheral attached to the top of the monitor. The challenge is that if your computer is compromised by malware, the malware can turn on the camera and use it to spy on you without your knowledge. While this unauthorized monitoring may or may not be a big deal in your office, it could be embarrassing for a personal machine located in your home or bedroom.

To control your PC camera, you should do the following:

– **Assess the risk of being recorded.** Your computer or device camera can be on and recording at any time. While many cameras have lights to indicate when they are recording, those lights are controlled by software and can be disabled by malicious software to deceive you. Turn on your camera and look at what it can see. What room is it in? What is in the background? What is visible in the camera if you are not sitting in front of it? Are you okay if all of this information gets recorded and broadcast to the world?

– **Beware of what you record.** If you post video to the internet, consider carefully what you are recording. Is there a family picture on the wall behind you that shows your spouse and kids? Is there a diploma on the wall that shows what school you went to? Do not hold up a bill or a prescription bottle in front of the camera, as they may contain your name, address, and phone number. With high definition, all the above items may be visible on your recording using freeze frame capabilities, video enhancement, etc. Internet "trolls" look for just this type of information online and use it to harass people, even if the victims have not done anything wrong.

- **Cover up your camera.** While we can never be sure if our camera is truly "off," covering up the lens means that even if it is on it can not see anything. When you are not using it, cover your camera lens with an opaque cover to be completely sure it is not being used without your knowledge.

Backing Up Your Operating System

Despite all of our security protection efforts, things still go wrong with our computer's operating system, applications, and data. Be prepared! Even if you have all of your software, disks, and files, rebuilding a corrupted computer can take hours of time. A "full system backup" to an external hard drive enables you to rapidly recover your computer, programs, and files, if something goes disastrously wrong. Backup storage is cheap compared to the cost of the time required to recover and rebuild a corrupted computer.

To back up your operating system, you should do the following:
- **Keep track of your software keys.** Sometimes doing a system restore may cause software to need to be re-enabled, especially if your hardware has changed. Keep track of your software keys, so you can reactivate your software if necessary.
- **Buy an external hard drive.** While there are advantages to online backups that make copies of your files every day and are immediately available for restoration, these services do not protect you from ransomware or malware corruption that destroy all of your connected data. Buy one or two inexpensive external drives to keep your backups away from your machine. Better—keep one of them in a safe deposit box.
- **Back up your entire computer.** Make a backup of your entire computer including the operating system, programs, and files. Sometimes this is called a "bare metal" or "system restore" backup.
- **Make a second backup of just your files.** In addition to a bare metal system restore backup, periodically make a backup copy of just your files, so they are available to you separately. This file backup can be easier to work with if you just need to recover a single file or folder that was lost off your primary system. This file backup is also helpful for archive files like old photographs.

- **Protect your backups.** Password protect your backups so if they are stolen or fall into someone else's hands they will not be usable. Make sure you know the password well and can remember it years later, should you need it.
- **Use online backups.** In addition to isolated offline storage that is protected from corruption or malicious attack, you can also use cloud-based subscription services like Google Drive, Dropbox, or Microsoft OneDrive. These services store your data "in the cloud" and can protect you from natural disasters such as a house fire or flood.
- **Have multiple copies.** Remember, if your data is precious, there should be more than one copy. If it is important, have at least two copies. If it is really important have at least three copies. If it is sensitive, encrypt all the copies. Do not let a mishap or mistake destroy your digital life.
- **Be aware of system restore.** Modern operating systems like Windows or MacOS include the ability to "system restore" or restore the operating system back to a known good state. Some of these features can reset the operating system while preserving your files, while others may delete your files or, more likely, your programs. Be aware of these features and understand how they can help you if there is a problem with your system.

Watching for Signs of Compromise

There is a joke on the internet where they show two identical pictures of computers, and ask the reader to identify which of them has been hacked. The fact is that there is no outward appearance change when your computer has been compromised or is under the control of an attacker. However, there are subtle signs that you can watch for to detect if something has gone wrong with your computer. If you see these signs, you should be prepared to completely restore your computer from a known good backup, or to do a "system restore" and reinstall your programs and data manually.

To watch for signs of compromise, you should consider the following:
- **Unexpected pop-up messages.** A normal operating system should almost never pop up a window telling you to do something. For the most part, legitimate operating system notification windows are designed to stay in the background and only bother you if there is an emergency. Pop-up messages for ransomware, antivirus software, or telling you to purchase something are all signs that your computer has been infected, or has opened a malicious website or page. If a phone number pops up on your screen, do not call the number.

- **Changes to your web browser.** Malware frequently changes your web browser. Changes might include changing your default web browser, installing plug-ins or toolbars to your web browser, or changing your search settings. If your browser has been changed or re-configured, you may have malware.
- **Programs you did not install.** Malware packages frequently include additional software packages above and beyond the original program. For example, you install a piece of freeware and then it installs a half-dozen other programs at the same time. Sometimes these programs are legitimate support code, but frequently they are malicious.
- **E-mails you did not send.** Malware packages may attempt to send e-mails to your friends and contacts purporting to be you. Worse, these e-mails frequently contain advertising links, links to malicious websites, or malware attachments. If your friends bring to your attention that you have been sending them unsolicited e-mails, your computer or e-mail account may have been hacked.
- **Your online passwords are changed.** If you find that you can not get into online accounts even though you are sure you have the passwords right, it is a sign that your computer or accounts may have been hacked. Attackers who have access to your e-mail accounts may use password reset features to take control of your online accounts. They may also cover their tracks by going into your e-mail account and deleting messages intended to notify you of the changes.
- **Online protections are disabled.** Malware packages frequently disable online protections like antimalware software. If you find that your antimalware software has been inexplicably turned off or is turned back off after you have turned it on, that is a sign your computer has been infected.
- **System programs stop working.** Similarly, malware packages frequently disable software tools like the Task Manager or Registry Editor (in Windows), or similar tools in MacOS or Linux. Disabling these software tools makes it harder for you to troubleshoot your system, or to disable the malware and manually remove it.
- **Unexpected startup programs.** When you first start your computer, there will be a flurry of activity as everything turns on, and then your computer should be relatively idle, waiting for you to do something. Open the Task Manager (Windows), Activity Monitor (MacOS), or System Monitor (Linux) to see what applications are currently active or running. There are related tools that tell you what programs are configured to automatically start every time you reboot your computer. Look over the list to see if there are unusual programs running, or programs using lots of system resources. If there are, research them to make sure they are legitimate.

- **High central processing unit (CPU) or disk usage.** Similarly, if your computer is working hard when you are not actively doing anything, such activity is a sign that unwanted software may be running. For example, malicious "cryptoware" uses your computer resources (e.g., storage and computing capabilities) without your permission to perform cryptomining calculations. Such unauthorized activity may be obvious due to its high resource usage, which slows down your computer.
- **Fraudulent posts or transactions.** If you find fraudulent posts on your social media accounts, or fraudulent transactions in your banking or e-commerce accounts, such activities are signs your computer or accounts may have been hacked.

Using Mac and Linux Operating Systems

"No, your Mac isn't immune to malware."

— Washington Post

Much of the discussion surrounding malicious software focuses on malware targeting the Microsoft Windows operating system. Just as the American bank robber Willie Sutton famously commented he robbed banks because "that's where the money is," most malware targets Windows because that's what most people use. MacOS and Linux operating systems are also large, complex software packages just like Windows, and have their own flaws and vulnerabilities that can be exploited by malicious software. Therefore, major malware and ransomware campaigns include versions of their software for MacOS and Linux operating systems, as well as Windows.

With the above comments in mind, if you use MacOS or Linux operating systems, you should do the following to protect your computer system:
- **Enjoy the fact that you are "less" vulnerable.** While you are hardly invulnerable, you are at least somewhat less vulnerable as the majority of malware is written to specifically target Windows. Only the more advanced malware packages typically target your less-common computer platforms.
- **Be cautious and vigilant.** Make sure you are running a modern, supported operating system and programs, and patch them promptly. You still need to be cautious surfing the web, opening attachments, and installing programs. Websites you visit, e-mails you open, and programs you install can all potentially be malicious.

-   **Bad things can still happen.** All the cyber protection in the world does not protect you from coffee spilled on a laptop computer, or a failed hard drive on a desktop computer. Backup your system and be prepared in case a disaster occurs.

Chapter 4
Protecting Your Passwords

After protecting your computer, the next most important thing you can do to protect yourself is to consider your online passwords. Most of us have a dizzying number of online accounts and passwords, and struggle to keep track of them all. Your list of websites, e-mail addresses, and passwords is the modern cyber keychain. Unfortunately, even though this keychain is virtual, the stakes are real. Passwords protect your data, your messaging, your contacts, your software, your commerce, and if you bank online, your money. You must take passwords seriously and treat them like the "virtual keys" they are.

This chapter discusses some ways in which you can create, manage, and protect your passwords to computers and the internet.

How Do Cyberattackers Get Your Password?

Cyberattackers can get your password using several different techniques. Good password practice consists of thwarting each of these techniques in sequence. Good password practice does not make it impossible for attackers to guess or otherwise obtain your passwords. After all, sometimes we have a bad day, or the attackers have a good day. Criminal aggregators have created lists of millions of users and their passwords, and likely have a couple of entries in a database on you, too. However, good practice improves your odds, and can also reduce the damage that occurs if one of your passwords is compromised.

Some ways that attackers can obtain your passwords include:
- **Brute force attack.** It is theoretically possible to "guess" any password by simply trying every combination of letters and numbers until you get the right combination. An eight-character password can be brute forced in less than 10 minutes using a distributed botnet, based on a 2017 report. Adding a character to your password increases this time by a factor of fifty or more, so longer passwords become significantly more difficult to crack. Websites and applications thwart brute force attacks by introducing a delay after each unsuccessful password attempt, or by locking accounts after a certain number of unsuccessful login attempts.
- **Rainbow tables.** Rainbow tables are huge tables containing millions of data entries that can be used to try to guess a user's password. There are also password lookup tables that contain millions of common password strings. These

DOI 10.1515/9781501506505-004

tables generally include all the words in the dictionary, along with common substitutions for those words like adding a number to the end or replacing the letter "a" with the "@" symbol.

- **Online hack databases.** Major hacks like those at Yahoo, Adobe, Experian, LinkedIn, and others may have revealed usernames and passwords for millions of internet users. The revealed account information is now contained in databases that are freely available within the criminal underworld. In response to some of these breaches, the Australian web security expert, Troy Hunt, created the website www.haveibeenpwned.com to allow users to check their accounts against some of these databases. While not being on this list does not mean you are in the clear, if you are on this list, then your password has most probably been compromised at some point.
- **Company breach.** If your company—or any company you work with—has been breached, it is likely that your password at that company has been compromised as well. Attackers frequently try to obtain authentication databases (e.g., usernames and passwords) from companies they breach. Even if they have not gotten your actual password, they may have obtained your password *hash*, which may be used to impersonate you or to obtain your actual password, under certain circumstances.
- **Keyloggers.** Similarly, if attackers compromise your computer, your phone, or a computer that you have used—like a public computing kiosk —then they may have obtained your credentials using a *keylogger*. Keyloggers are programs that monitor and record what keystrokes are entered via the keyboard, while looking for certain patterns that indicate a password is being entered. For example, a keylogger may watch for you to go to common logon pages or watch for you to type patterns like "user@domain.com." These patterns may indicate you are entering an e-mail address, followed by a password.
- **Network sniffing.** Like keylogging, attackers can watch network traffic for credentials as well. While proper implementations encrypt usernames and passwords before they are sent over the internet or wireless connections, it is not always the case. Implementation glitches may allow these credentials to be transmitted in the clear, or poor encryption may permit attackers to decrypt the credentials and obtain the usernames and passwords.
- **Shoulder surfing.** Usually, the people most likely to be looking over our shoulder as we are entering passwords are our family or friends, but that is not always the case. In public with a laptop, at an ATM, or while sitting in front of a client, people who you do not know well may have opportunities to see what you type and may just try it themselves out of curiosity or malice. Be situationally aware every time you type your password and shield your fingers if you think you are being watched. One useful technique is to type

wrong characters in the middle of the password and then backspace over them—this makes it hard for others to follow what you actually ended up typing.

Do Not Use a Bad Password

Appendix B contains a list of 20 of the "worst passwords of 2017" from Splash-Data. Tripwire reports that "123456" is the worst password of all time. Look over these lists and do not be one of these users! What you see on these lists is that passwords consisting of common words, sequential numbers, and basic keyboard patterns like "qwerty" are well-known among cyberattackers. Such passwords are among the first passwords to be successfully guessed by an attacker trying to get access to your computer. The professional attackers are not going to try to breach your passwords one at a time. They are going to write scripts that test hundreds, thousands, or millions of passwords, without any manual intervention.

To avoid using bad passwords, you should consider the following:
- **Avoid dictionary words.** The first list attackers use is the dictionary. On UNIX computers, there is a file called "usr/share/dict/words" that is automatically installed and contains over 200,000 English words, along with word lists in other common languages as well.
- **Avoid names and dates.** Like the dictionary, there are lists of common first and last names, as well as the complete results of the U.S. Census, all available online. Dates, with their strict formats of MM/DD/YYYY, or MM-DD-YYYY or DD-MMM-YYYY, are easily generated by a computer program and tested en masse.
- **Avoid obvious permutations.** Since attackers are hacking passwords with a computer, it is easy to do simple permutations of those words. These permutations might include replacing "a" with "@," "l" with "1" (that is the letter and the number), or other common adjustments, as well as adding numbers or punctuation marks to the ends of words. Similar techniques can be used with a telephone keypad to guess PIN codes.

Create Good Passwords and Passphrases

There is an art to creating good passwords. Good passwords are hard to guess, easy to remember, comply with password policies for applications and websites, and are not in password databases. While it is useful to be able to memorize your passwords, it is more important that passwords be strong than for them to be memorized. The challenge here is passwords that are written down or stored somewhere are vulnerable if that storage is breeched. It's all about managing tradeoffs. An insecure password that you can remember is probably a less secure choice than a secure password that you store in your phone or web browser (provided your phone or web browser is kept secure).

To create good passwords and passphrases, you should consider the following:
- **Make it long enough.** Make sure your password is long enough to resist brute-force attacks. It used to be that 8 characters was enough—today it is more like 10, 12, or 14 characters. Longer is better. There is nothing wrong with having a password that is 20 characters or more, provided it works with the technology or website involved.
- **Make it complex enough.** Complexity and length go together. By adding in uppercase, lowercase, numbers, and punctuation you ensure your password is not in a dictionary attack. Also, most applications and websites require complexity.
- **Make it easy to remember.** A good password is easy to remember. While names or dates on their own may be insecure, a combination of elements (like a name, plus a date, plus a random string, plus complexity) can still be simple while also being secure. Including the name of a website along with other secure password elements allows you to make a password unique to that site without having to think of random strings.
- **Watch out for password policies.** Common applications and websites have their own password policies and requirements, and they can vary widely. These policies can make creating passwords more challenging, as some sites require punctuation, while other sites require capitalization, etc. In addition, sites may have limitations like not allowing spaces or quotation marks. Minimum and maximum password length requirements vary widely.
- **Consider passphrases.** A passphrase involves stringing together a series of words, dates, numbers, or names into a "phrase" and then using that phrase as your password. A phrase can also include punctuation and numbers within the context of the phrase. Just beware that long passphrases with spaces may not work at some sites and may also be difficult to type on mobile devices.
- **Make "families" of passwords.** Using the tips above, you should consider creating "families" of passwords and passphrases that all use a consistent pattern that you can remember easily, while also being related in a way that only you know. This technique allows you to rapidly change passwords when necessary to other passwords in the "family" and to group passwords according to their function, their use, or the password policies of the sites

involved. You might have passwords that are optimized to be more secure, to be easier to remember (like for a family Wi-Fi site), or to be longer or more complex. You would then choose the appropriate password for the appropriate application.

- **Make use of password hints.** Many applications and websites have password "hints" that you can use to help jog your memory if you forget the password. Do not just put "the usual" in these fields. Use these fields to identify the general password policy or the password family that you used for this site, so you can reconstruct in your memory or your notes what the correct password should be.

Rotate Passwords Regularly

Even the best password is bound to be compromised sometime, and once a password is on a breach database, it should be considered compromised forever. Websites like www.haveibeenpwned.com have taken some of these databases and made them available so the public can check their e-mail address usernames to see if they have been compromised. However, these tools are not complete. Even the best password "ages" and becomes less secure the longer it is in place and the more it is used.

To rotate your passwords regularly, you should consider the following:

- **Change your passwords quarterly, or at least annually.** In general, you should try to change your passwords at least once a year, and preferably once a quarter.
- **Change your passwords after a breach.** Obviously, if you hear of a breach at a website you frequent, or at one of your accounts, you should change your password. If you reuse a password at multiple sites and one of them is compromised, you should change your password at *all* of them. Attackers will frequently try stolen passwords across multiple sites, because they know users often re-use passwords.
- **Change your passwords after suspicious use.** If you detect suspicious use of your account, or signs your account has been tampered with, one of your first steps should be to change your password for that account.
- **Change your passwords after international travel.** Most of us do not think about this regularly, but you should change your passwords if you used them while traveling internationally or using public kiosks or open networks. In some countries, your logons might be monitored by national intelligence agencies, if you are identified as being a foreigner.

- **Consider automatic password management.** The easiest way to regularly change your password is to have a machine do it for you. Password management tools can randomly generate passwords for you and automatically change your passwords on a regular basis. Automatic password rotation can make passwords secure and extremely resistant to attack, especially for sensitive financial transactions or systems administration.

Avoid Sharing Passwords

A common approach for managing password complexity is to come up with one good password, memorize it, and then use that password everywhere. *This single password approach is a bad idea!* You need to avoid sharing passwords or, if you are going to share passwords, do so carefully and with caution.

To avoid sharing passwords, you should consider the following:
- **Reduce the number of places where you share passwords.** While perhaps overly simplistic, this password advice is good general guidance. It is much better for you to use password families to create unique but easy-to-remember passwords for each application or website.
- **Use unique passwords for shared applications.** When you have an application where multiple people will access the password—like your home Wi-Fi, family Netflix, or other account—use a password that is unique from your other passwords. Most likely you will want this password to be easier to remember and type, as well.
- **Do not share between high security and low security needs.** Your best passwords should be reserved for your highest security applications, such as e-mail, cell phone, e-commerce, and financial accounts. E-mail and cell phone accounts need strong passwords because attackers can use them to force password resets to other accounts and get into your applications, despite your passwords.
- **Password management is sharing, too.** When you click "remember this password" in your web browser, or use a password management tool, you are basically sharing the password with that application. While these applications include security features, they are not impregnable. Your most important passwords should be shared as little as possible—it is best if they can be memorized and never shared at all.
- **Know where passwords are written down, cached, or recorded.** When you write a password down, click "remember this password" in your web browser, or store it in a password manager, it becomes vulnerable. A breach

to any of those locations can compromise the password. Know where you are recording your passwords, so if there is a problem you know which passwords need to be reset and changed.

Change Default Passwords

Just as shared passwords can pose a risk to your security, default passwords pose an even greater risk. Default passwords can appear on websites, in applications, or on network-connected devices. Most frequently, they appear on network-connected devices like routers, Wi-Fi access points, and internet of things (IoT) devices like locks, printers, gaming consoles, and home appliances.

To change default passwords, you should consider the following:
- **Know where default passwords reside.** When you purchase computers, applications, services, or network-connected devices, read the documentation and check to see if there are default passwords. Devices like internet routers frequently have their default passwords printed on a sticker attached to the device.
- **Change default passwords.** When you find default passwords, go ahead and change them, consistent with good password practices.
- **Rotate these passwords at least occasionally.** Especially for devices that are internet-facing or connect to the internet, you should rotate the passwords occasionally. Also make sure these devices are kept up-to-date with their firmware and software.

Safeguard Your Passwords

The challenge of having lots of passwords is keeping them safe while also having them at your fingertips when you need them. While a sticky note under your keyboard may be relatively safe, it is not convenient when you are on travel, nor does it scale well to support hundreds of accounts. To safeguard your passwords, you need to balance competing priorities of security, convenience, robustness, protection, and accessibility.

To safeguard your passwords, you should consider the following:
- **Memorize the most important passwords.** While not every password needs to be memorized, the ones that protect your safety and your money are

probably more important than others. Keep track of the handful of passwords that are most important to you and commit those passwords to memory.

- **Consider keeping a "master password" list.** For the rest of your passwords, it may be desirable to keep track of them in a password list or password organizer. This list can be on paper, or it can be on a device. Paper lists have the advantage of being impossible to hack, while they are vulnerable in other ways. Mobile phones are good places to keep lists electronically, since they are convenient and are frequently more secure from hacking than personal computers.

- **Protect your master password list.** If you keep your master list on the computer or on a device like a smartphone, make sure it is protected as well. Use password or biometric protection so only you can access the list. Also make sure the password list is backed up in case your device is lost or compromised.

- **Keep your passwords separate from your computer.** By having your passwords on your phone, but primarily using them on the computer, you reduce the risk of computer compromise resulting in account compromise (but just a little). Avoid keeping your passwords "in the clear" on your computer, or in cloud-based storage like Dropbox. Use encryption so your passwords are protected even if the file they are in is obtained by someone.

- **Use a password manager.** Password manager tools usually include encryption to protect your password list, authentication to verify it is you, and may include cloud storage in case you lose your device or to synchronize passwords across multiple devices. These services are not impregnable, but their benefits generally outweigh their risks.

- **Have backup plans.** No matter how good or secure your password management is, things go wrong. Losing access to some web postings may not be a big deal but losing ten years of personal photos may be. Consider the accounts you use and have backup plans for access, in case your passwords are lost or compromised.

Understand Password Reset Mechanisms

An internet developer once famously joked, "Password reset *is* an authentication method." The ability to reset your password has long been a poorly-understood backdoor of internet security, and only recently have defenders begun giving it the attention it deserves. The challenge is that if it is easier to reset your password than it is to guess it, then resetting becomes the bigger vulnerability. Rather than try to guess, brute-force, or hack your account, attackers simply pretend to be you and reset the password to something they know. Frequently, by the time you figure out it has happened; the attackers are long gone.

To understand password reset vulnerabilities, you should consider the following:
- **Know your password reset mechanisms.** For your most important accounts, check how their password reset mechanism works. Password reset is often dependent on other accounts, like e-mail accounts or phone numbers, to authenticate you. Make sure this information is kept up-to-date, and that you have alternatives, such as if you lose your phone.
- **Secure e-mail accounts used for password reset.** Most often, password reset involves sending a temporary link or password to your e-mail account. Make sure this account is as well-protected as the accounts it is securing. Also, make sure you have a password reset mechanism for the e-mail account set up.
- **Secure phone numbers used for password reset.** Telephone short message service (SMS) (also known as, texting) or phone identification is an increasingly popular mechanism for password reset, as well as for multifactor authentication (see below). Professional attackers may try to hijack your phone to reset your password and may be able to do so if they get online access to your cell phone provider. Protect this account as well as your most secure e-mail and financial accounts.
- **Watch for password reset notifications.** Watch out for signs that your passwords have been reset. Attackers who are resetting your passwords may try to cover their tracks by deleting notification messages or hiding them so you can not see them. When you logon to accounts, watch for messages that state when you last logged in, or that a new computer has connected to your account. These messages could all be signs your account has been hijacked.

Use Multifactor Authentication

Regardless of how strong your password is, the strongest password in the world is most likely less secure than multifactor authentication. Multifactor authentication involves using something you *have*, in addition to the password you *know*, to positively identify you online. The thing you have may be a smart card, a digital fob (i.e., security token), a universal serial bus (USB) device, an app on your phone, or a biometric property such as your face or fingerprint. While multifactor authentication is widely used to secure workplace applications, it is becoming more common for financial and e-mail accounts as well. Not all accounts, applications, or websites support multifactor authentication, but some of your most important ones probably do.

To use multifactor authentication, you should consider the following:
- **Know what accounts support multifactor.** Check your most important financial and e-mail accounts to see if they support multifactor authentication and use it where you can. Also, multifactor may work on mobile apps, but not work for web access, or vice versa. Understand the fine print and make sure that multifactor authentication works for you.
- **Understand cards, tokens, fobs, and apps.** Multifactor includes a variety of form factors, with different limitations and considerations for each. You may encounter smart cards, one-time-password tokens, USB fobs, smartphone applications, and biometrics. There is no "one-size-fits-all" with multifactor authentication.
- **Keep your second factors together.** The power of multifactor authentication is that you should notice if your second factor is lost or stolen. So, keep your authentication devices together so you know where they are. A keychain may be useful, or keeping them in a locked drawer. Just make sure you know where they are and that they are all present.
- **Have a backup plan.** Multifactor authentication introduces a whole new way to get locked out of your accounts. Make sure you understand the backup options and reset mechanisms in case you lose your token or get locked out of your account. Beware that when multifactor is enabled, password reset mechanisms may also be enhanced to make your account harder to hack. These security features may make it harder for you to get in, as well.

Chapter 5
Protecting Your Home Network

When you are at home or work, the network itself is your first line of defense against attack by hackers, malware, or other attacks. In the past, a home computer network might consist of one or two personal computers connected to the home router by a physical cable. As shown in Figure 5.1, today, a home computer network may consist of a dozen or more internet of things (IoT) devices all connected to the home computer network wirelessly and providing for streaming TV (e.g., Netflix, Amazon on Demand, Hulu), automated door locks, physical security monitoring systems, climate control, refrigerator monitoring, home health, and other functions.

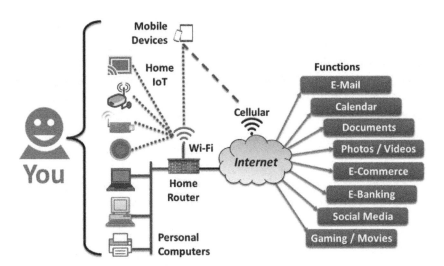

Figure 5.1: Home computer networks are increasingly capable and correspondingly complex.

Your home network gives you a safe place to connect devices, surf the web, read documents, and conduct commerce. But a home network is not impregnable. Vulnerabilities, compromised devices, and irresponsible behavior can all neutralize the protection of the home network.

This chapter describes a home networking environment, and how you can configure it for security against attack, inside and out. Some of this chapter may be somewhat technical as we have chosen to be comprehensive. By reading

DOI 10.1515/9781501506505-005

through it, you can understand the issues and options you have relating to your home network cyber defense.

Checking Your Network Modem, Router, and Firewall

Home networks typically consist of a high-speed wired connection to the internet, and then components plugged into that connection. Not all environments have all these components, and some environments may have significantly more components. Typical wired internet connections use optical fiber, coaxial cable, or telephone wires. Wireless connections are also available, using satellite or cellular technology. These connections terminate in one or more devices that act as *modems*, *routers*, and/or *firewalls* for the network. They often also include Wi-Fi capability.

Your home network is typically set up for you by your internet service provider (ISP) as part of establishing service. While you should not have to second-guess the ISP's work, going into the configuration of these devices may give you access to additional security capabilities, while also introducing the risk of misconfiguring those capabilities. Use caution changing these settings unless you really know what you are doing.

To check your network modem, router, and firewall, you should consider the following:

– **Check your devices for vulnerabilities.** Know the manufacturer and model numbers of your network connection devices, and search the internet to see if they have been discontinued, found to be vulnerable, or otherwise compromised. If internet commentary indicates they are "unsafe" you may be able to contact your ISP and ask for an update or a replacement. If you can update the firmware to your device, make sure the firmware is up-to-date.
– **Disable remote administration.** Network modems and routers frequently allow remote administration from the internet, protected by a username and password. First, *make sure that remote administration is disabled*, unless you have a significant need for it (or really trust your ISP). Remote management is often turned off by default, but discuss remote management options with your ISP if you need them. If remote management is enabled, make sure it is protected by a username and strong password that you create. A default username and password such as "admin" and "password" should be changed, unless there is a compelling reason to leave them alone.
– **Be aware of network address translation.** Network address translation, (NAT) is your primary line of defense protecting your home network. NAT

configures your home's local area network (LAN) to use "private" network addresses that do not work across the internet's public wide area network (WAN). Your computers and devices on your home network use the private addresses internally to protect against external attacks from the internet. NAT also enables a device, such as a router, to translate the private addresses to public addresses so you can communicate between your home network and the internet. ISPs generally enable NAT for home networks by default; contact your ISP if you have questions or concerns.

-   **Configure network firewalls.** Similarly, your router's firewall should also be enabled by default. The firewall means your router will not respond if it is probed by the internet, except when those probes match certain allowed ports, protocols, or other patterns. The firewall may also provide additional protection like filtering what protocols can connect to the internet, and allowing or blocking certain remote internet addresses.
-   **Check wireless networking or Wi-Fi configuration.** If your devices provide you with a home Wi-Fi hotspot (most do), check that configuration as well. More on this topic in the next section.
-   **Do not allow remote access.** Many home routers allow remote access, so you can connect to your home network while you are on travel. While powerful, these features are easy to mis-configure to allow your home network to be "wide open" to attack. Be cautious if you choose to use these features.

Securing Your Wi-Fi Configuration

Wi-Fi has been through several revisions over the years, generally indicated by letters—A, B, G, N, and AC—and has steadily increased speed and bandwidth with each subsequent revision. Because of its popularity, Wi-Fi has been thoroughly tested for security, and is generally robust when configured properly. However, some would argue that most of its security comes from its short range, since attackers must be within a hundred feet or so to connect. Just as your neighborhood provides a lot of the security protecting your home, the Wi-Fi short-range capability limits the number of people who might attack it. However, the short-range capability does not make Wi-Fi immune to attack.

Unlike many internet technologies, the Wi-Fi protocols have not been so seriously compromised that older networking devices are *completely* unsafe. However, vulnerabilities have been found over the years, and many devices run versions of the Wi-Fi protocols that may be targeted and attacked. Successful attack against your Wi-Fi network may mean attackers get a copy of your wireless logon password, can join your wireless network, or can "sniff" wireless traffic between wireless devices and the network. This traffic can also include other logons and passwords, if those are sent in the clear and not protected separately by their own encryption.

To secure your Wi-Fi configuration, and if you are technically able to do so, you should consider the following:

– **Become familiar with your Wi-Fi router's administrative console.** To check to see who is accessing your Wi-Fi you need to log into the router's administrative console. If you have not already logged into your console, you will need to get your router's IP address.

1. For Windows, enter "cmd" in the Start menu on your desktop and then type "ipconfig" in the Command Prompt window that appears.

2. Find the listing for the "Default Gateway" IP address. Frequently, it is "192.168.0.1" or "192.168.1.1" but it may be something else entirely.

3. In your web browser, type in the address "http://<IP address>" where "<IP address>" is the address you looked up in the previous step. If that does not work, try "https://<IP address>."

4. You should then be prompted for a username and password. Frequently, the username is "admin" and the password is "password" but that may not be the case. The username and password may be printed on a label on the router, or contained in the router's documentation.

5. After entering your credentials, look for something like "connected devices" to see what/who is connected to your Wi-Fi router. Look at the connected devices to determine if you recognize the users or devices.

6. If you think you have unauthorized users, change the Wi-Fi password and let the authorized users know the new password so they can access your network.

7. Alternatively, you can segment the unrecognized devices away from the main network by following the online instructions.

– **Check your Wi-Fi protocols.** Wi-Fi protocols have held up relatively well over time, but there are revisions to those protocols to correct bugs and improve security. Check your devices (e.g., computers, tablets, smart TVs, and printers) to determine if they support the standards used by your Wi-Fi router. Use the latest Wi-Fi protocol—802.11ac—where practical. Watch out for press coverage indicating that an older protocol is "unsafe." If an older protocol is thought to be unsafe, consider disabling that protocol. Typically, if you are experiencing "poor" Wi-Fi connectivity or performance and have a combination of both new and old devices, consider upgrading to a new router that supports the latest Wi-Fi standards.

- **Enable Wi-Fi security.** Configure your Wi-Fi with security and encryption enabled, and choose the strongest available encryption. Today, the current encryption is "WPA2" (Wi-Fi Protected Access 2). WPA2 has vulnerabilities that are planned to be addressed in a future "WPA3" standard. When newer security standards come out, consider upgrading to them if possible.
- **Configure a strong password.** Configure a strong, but easy-to-remember, password for your Wi-Fi network. Network-connected devices like game systems, home assistants, or appliances may necessitate a simpler password than you might prefer. Strike a reasonable balance and change the password periodically.
- **Segment your network.** If you have older devices on your network that are not very secure, vulnerable, or require a less-secure Wi-Fi network configurations, consider setting up a separate "segmented" network. Many routers can support multiple Wi-Fi networks or can allow for primary and guest networks. Putting less secure devices onto a separate Wi-Fi network can reduce your risk, without impairing their ability to operate.
- **Consider what is "in range."** To hack your Wi-Fi, an attacker must be within range of your access point. Typically, this range is less than a hundred feet, but the range depends on several factors. In a residential neighborhood, your range may only extend to the edges of your property, while in an apartment building your range may extend to more than a dozen neighbors. Hackers with directional antennas may be able to connect to your Wi-Fi from a mile away.
- **Watch out for secondary networks.** Some home devices may generate their own Wi-Fi networks, in addition to connecting to your home network. Be careful that these devices are not providing a backdoor into your supposedly secure network. When in doubt, segment these devices away from the main network.
- **Periodically check your network.** Using your Wi-Fi administrative console, you should occasionally check your network to make sure has not been changed without your knowledge. Your console should have a section related to your network protocols and security settings. You should check them to make sure they are still enabled and up-to-date. You should also check with your device manufacturer for updates to its firmware or configuration settings.

Supporting Visitors and Guests

Most of us have house guests who ask to use our Wi-Fi for their computer, phone, gaming console, or smartwatch. But how secure is the device we are letting them connect? Is it free of malware? Is it malicious? Is it connected to other devices? We do not want to be rude, but we also do not know much about these devices we are allowing inside our network. Once they connect to our internal Wi-Fi network, they have unfettered access to everything else on our home network, unless that home network has been segmented for additional protection.

To reduce this risk, most modern Wi-Fi access points include features to establish a "guest network" for just this purpose. You can use your Wi-Fi router's administrative console to set up a guest network by following the router documentation. Such networks usually provide guests with internet access, while limiting their ability to connect to the rest of the host's home network. This approach is usually a good balance of functionality with security and eliminates the need to ask your guests awkward questions about their internet surfing habits or computer administration hygiene.

To securely support visitors and guests, you should consider the following:

– **Enable guest networking.** Enable guest networking on your home network. If you have insecure network-connected devices or appliances, you may want to connect them to this network, rather than your regular home network. Check the guest network configuration to make sure it is segregated from your regular home network.

– **Configure a guest password.** Even though it is for guests, and is supposed to be "low security," configure a password for your guest network. The password does not have to be too high-security but should be enough to prevent casual access to the network without your knowledge or permission.

– **Periodically check your guest configuration.** Periodically check and reset your guest network configuration and change its password. It is okay to ask visitors to setup their devices with a new password if they only come to visit once a year.

Configuring Multimedia and Gaming Consoles

Internet-based multimedia is in the process of totally transforming how we consume content. Modern gaming consoles are another important, interactive, part of this multimedia experience. Streaming "sticks"—like Roku and Amazon Firestick—plug into your smart television so you can watch movies, TV episodes, and other media and are increasing in popularity. A property these devices share is they are basically full-featured computers masquerading as home appliances and provide us with rich two-way functionality through our home high-definition televisions. These devices have the capabilities of a personal computer, but only provide us a reduced interface, few administration tools, heavily concealed operating systems, and often no keyboard for typing cryptic or complex passwords.

These devices are not just about media or games, either. Smart TV's can let you not only watch content from services like Netflix or Hulu, but also conduct e-commerce using Amazon or eBay. You can store your credit cards for easy online purchases, along with your home shipping information. On gaming consoles, you can establish multiple online identities, and then link those identities to your accounts on PCs and mobile devices, along with payment information for purchasing in-game power-ups and bonus features. There is real commerce taking place on these devices, with real money at stake.

To securely configure multimedia and gaming consoles, you should consider the following:

- **Retire obsolete devices.** As fun as it may be to have an original Xbox on your home network, some of these older devices have been retired for some time. The older devices are no longer supported by the manufacturer and frequently have unpatched vulnerabilities that may be exploited by attackers. Retire your obsolete multimedia or gaming consoles, or at least disable their internet access.
- **Keep your devices up-to-date.** These devices frequently have an auto-update feature, and some of the better ones make sure they are up-to-date before they allow you to use them (although when this feature fails you may be out of luck). Make sure your devices are up-to-date, install all recommended patches, and use caution if you see media coverage of a major vulnerability.
- **Be aware of what accounts are on your devices.** Smart multimedia devices can frequently include more than a dozen different applications with which you can have accounts and relationships. Many of these applications are paid, while others, like e-mail, may be free. Make sure you know which accounts you have on which devices, and whether those accounts include payment information or not.
- **Pay attention to online gaming.** It is easy to set up an online gaming account for your kids and, before you know it, find out you have given them your credit card and free reign to charge to it. Use extreme caution when enabling payment capabilities within online games and educate your kids on your rules regarding making in-game purchases.

- **Put passwords on your multimedia devices.** As inconvenient as more passwords might be, if you are concerned that kids, guests, friends, or service personnel might be abusing your multimedia devices, passwords might be necessary. Use the features built in to your devices to "lock them down" so they can not be abused.

Protecting Home Internet of Things Devices and Smart Locks

As the revolution in network-connected multimedia devices has taken off, cheap computing has made it possible to build internet connectivity and network-connected smarts into more and more home devices. The modern connected home includes internet connections for doorbells, video cameras, baby monitors, alarm systems, thermostats, appliances, solar power, and even power strips. You can remotely unlock your doors, turn off your lights, change the temperature, and charge your Tesla car, all through your mobile phone or remote computer and enabled by your home network. But all this capability comes with risks. While each of these devices is as powerful as a personal computer of a generation ago, they may not be implemented, supported, or secured like one.

Modern internet of things (IoT) devices generally run a "stripped down" operating system, frequently based upon an open-source core like Linux or Android. These operating systems are then embedded into the devices, and may or may not be updatable after the device is shipped. Properties of these devices include: (1) protocols like Thread, ZigBee, Z-Wave, or KNX for communication; (2) smart "hubs" that may control multiple devices and permit you to interact with them; and (3) outside internet services for "anywhere" access to your smart home devices from your PC or smartphone. Some of these capabilities require Wi-Fi connectivity, while others use their own proprietary wireless connections. It all depends, and the details may be very complex.

To protect your home IoT devices and smart locks, you should consider the following:

- **Inventory your smart devices.** Understand the smart devices in your home, and how they connect. Your solar panel system may have its own wireless connection that plugs into your home internet. Think about smart appliances you installed years ago, or your kids' toys that are network-connected. It is important to know what in your home is "smart," how those devices connect inside and outside your home.
- **Know your device protocols.** For better or for worse, there are a myriad of home IoT device protocols and interfaces. While many devices use either

Wi-Fi or Bluetooth (which are well-known) these communication protocols are hardly the only protocols for IoT connectivity. Understand what protocols your devices use. If those protocols are not mainstream Wi-Fi or Bluetooth, research them to make sure they are secure enough for your purposes.

- **Watch out for the cloud.** Some of the most remarkable smart device capabilities, like voice recognition, rely upon sending everything you say or do to "the cloud" for analysis. This analysis then determines if you are talking to your refrigerator or gesturing to your television, and what the device should do about that behavior. While these capabilities are not entirely bad—there is nothing wrong with your television knowing when you wave at it—it may also involve invading your privacy in ways that you are not quite ready to consider. Read the fine print in your device manual and make your own decision on what is acceptable. A smart TV watching you in the living room might be okay, while the same surveillance in your bedroom might not be okay. In addition, you may also wish to disable automatic content recognition (ACR) features. These smart device features track your personal viewing activity and share it with manufacturers and advertisers, often without your knowledge or consent.
- **Secure your IoT devices.** If you use smart locks from one of the major manufacturers, do some research on those devices to make sure they are secure enough. If you find reputable articles indicating those devices are not safe or secure, consider replacing or upgrading them. Alternatively, if the manufacturer has released an update to improve security, install it. Understand when you embrace the "smart" home, you also incur an obligation to protect the home, as well. You must pay attention to your devices and keep them up-to-date and secure.
- **Retire insecure devices.** Unfortunately, "smart" devices do not have the same life cycles as their non-smart siblings or brethren. While it may be just fine to have a thirty-year-old lock on your front door (provided it has been rekeyed within the past ten years) having a decade-old smart lock is probably not a good idea. If your smart devices are no longer supported, obsolete, or just plain out-of-date, go ahead and let them go.
- **Manage your IoT risks.** On the one hand, the press is going to sensationalize if a researcher finds a way to defeat an internet-connected lock. On the other hand, lock pickers have dozens of ways to defeat the typical home lock's key and tumblers, and those techniques seldom get any press coverage at all. To say nothing of breaking a window or forcing an entry. Just because your IoT is less than perfect does not mean you should throw it out—just understand the risk and consider that risk alongside the other risks in your life.

Understanding Remote Access and Running Your Own Servers

One of the more advanced features of home networking routers is the ability to allow remote access to your home network. Another advanced feature is the ability to set up your own server for home networking, internet gaming, or other purposes. While it is neat to be able to access your home network and services from everywhere, these capabilities open your home network up to all sorts of advanced attacks from the internet. While we are not going to tell you *not* to do these things, we recommend extreme caution and careful attention to detail.

Running remote access or your own servers can be very hazardous to your home network and are outside the scope of this book.

If you intend to enable remote access or run your own servers, you should consider the following:
- **Do your research.** Companies spend millions of dollars standing up internet-facing servers, databases, and applications, yet still get hacked. If you intend to enable these services, you need to consider devices, protocols, applications, interfaces, and authentication. A single mistake could be disastrous.
- **Enable security and encryption.** Enable the security features built into your internet-facing services and servers. Security features include encryption capabilities like Secure Sockets Layer (SSL) or Transport Layer Security (TLS)—along with server certificates—that provide communication security over a network. Once you have turned these features on, you will need to consider protocol versions for web browsing, e-mail, and other communications; corresponding vulnerabilities; and appropriate patches to keep them up-to-date and secure on an ongoing basis.
- **Require authentication.** Most likely if you are enabling remote access or running your own servers, they are for a closed community and not the public at large. To enforce this access restriction, you need to set up accounts for your users and authentication for those accounts. You also need to configure your systems to protect against password attacks like rainbow tables and brute force. You may also want to consider employing advanced, multifactor authentication.
- **Regularly check logs and configurations.** When you are internet-facing, you will be scanned daily by attackers using advanced automated tools to try to take over your systems. While these scans themselves are not a big deal, any exploit of your system is. Periodically check your logs and your configurations to make sure your system remains secure and is only being accessed by the expected users. Check your system documentation and the internet for guidance on which logs should be checked and how to check them.

Chapter 6
Smartphones and Tablets

Modern smartphones are amazing pieces of equipment. More powerful than a 1990s supercomputer, they are small, convenient, energy-efficient, and come with built-in peripherals like touch screens, motion sensors, global positioning system (GPS), cameras, and of course, cellular connectivity. Perhaps most remarkable is their energy efficiency, which permits them to send and receive messages, watch movies, and talk on the phone for hours, all on a single charge. Modern smartphones and their larger cousins, tablets, are so successful that many users have dispensed with personal computers altogether, doing all their computing on their phones.

Delivering the power of a personal computer to an object in your pocket has risks, however, as your smartphone can be targeted by attackers just like a personal computer. While smartphone infection rates are generally lower than that for personal computers, attackers are targeting them and infection rates are increasing. As with all things computing and internet-related, you should be vigilant and cautious as you use your devices to message, surf the web, communicate with your colleagues, and talk on the phone. And, of course, they are far more frequently lost or stolen than other, larger, computing devices.

This chapter describes smartphones and tablets, how they are different from personal computing, and how you can protect them at home and at work.

Smartphone and Tablet Differences

Phones and tablets have some significant differences that separate them from their larger PC cousins. Phones and tablets run different operating systems—most usually either iOS from Apple or Android from Google. While these operating systems were originally "stripped down" versions of larger computer operating systems, today's mobile operating systems are pretty much as fully-featured as their PC counterparts, supporting multitasking, external peripherals, keyboards, mice, and large external displays. Phones and tablets are somewhat slower than PCs, primarily because they are optimized for low power consumption.

Another difference lies in how you install applications onto phones and tablets. Whereas PC software may be delivered to you on a disk, or through an online download that you run, mobile software comes from app stores that are integrated with the operating systems and facilitate the installation process for you. The application stores ensure the applications you install abide by the stan-

DOI 10.1515/9781501506505-006

dards of the operating system, are compatible with your version of the operating system, and screen for potentially malicious behavior. While not perfect, these measures greatly reduce the amount of malicious software available for smartphones and tablets.

Another difference has to do with systems administration of smartphone and tablet operating systems. On a personal computer, the user is frequently the "administrator," able to not only install programs but also to manipulate and reconfigure the operating system at will. The computer has little protection against a malicious, negligent, or careless user reconfiguring it to turn off security protections. With mobile devices, however, the user does not have such systems administration privileges, limiting their ability to reconfigure the device or adjust the operating system (on mobile device operating systems, this is called "rooting"). While this administrative privilege restriction gets in the way of some desired activities like customizing icons, display formats, or built-in applications, it also provides significant protections to the device from unintentional operating system changes that jeopardize necessary functionality.

Another difference with smartphones and cellular-connected tablets has to do with the network. When a computer is connected to a home or work network, the "big, bad internet" is just outside the network firewall, and can be easily accessed either for good or for harm. When a smartphone is connected to the cellular network, it is connected to a private network operated by the cellular company. While the cellular companies do not stop your phone from being hacked, they do screen the network traffic in and out of the cellular network, and protect your phone from being scanned from the internet. The cellular companies may also block malware attempting to spread beyond your phone.

Protecting Your Smartphone or Tablet

Modern smartphones and tablets pack tremendous computing power, storage, and connectivity into a beautiful form factor that is, in some cases, entirely made out of glass. Drops, scratches, and bodies of water are ever-present threats to our mobile devices, with expensive and life-disrupting consequences. Also, if your phone is lost or stolen, a treasure trove of personal data contained on it becomes vulnerable to theft or abuse. Not only do you want your data to be safe from loss, but you need your personal data to be safe from compromise as well.

To protect your smartphone or tablet from loss, damage, or theft, you should consider the following:

- **PIN protect your device.** Put a screen lock on your device using a password, a personal identification number (PIN), biometric authentication, or facial recognition, so your device will be locked should it be lost or stolen. Lock screens also give you a space to put an emergency phone number or other personal information in case of an emergency or if a Good Samaritan should find your device.
- **Buy a case and screen protector.** Cases are available for almost every brand of smartphone or tablet, with varying levels of coverage and protection. Screen protectors can protect the device screen from scratches; hardened glass screen protectors can protect it from shattering as well.
- **Back up your device.** Assume your device will get lost, stolen, broken, or damaged. Consider using cloud services (protected by a strong password), so your photos and contacts are backed up when you create them. Regardless, make sure everything else important on your phone or tablet is backed up somewhere as well.
- **Set up "find my phone."** Mobile operating systems include features to allow you to locate your phone if it is lost or stolen, and also to remotely delete the data on your phone if it is connected to the cellular network. Activate these features to protect your data and privacy if your phone is stolen.
- **Consider insurance or ruggedized devices.** Phone carriers have insurance to cover device replacement if your device is lost or damaged. You may also be able to get similar coverage cheaper from phone manufacturers or third parties. Also, it used to be that ruggedized phones were relegated to niche industries like construction and the military, but now such phones are in the mainstream. Consider if your favorite phone platform is available in a ruggedized or water-resistant form factor that may survive the rigors of life.

Addressing Mobile Operating System Vulnerabilities

The Finnish telecommunications company Nokia reported in 2017 that they found mobile device infection rates to be 1.35%, or 135 infected mobile devices out of every 10,000. Considering that corresponding PC infection rates are typically between 10% and 30%, mobile device infection is a much smaller problem than it is for personal computers. There are a number of reasons for this lower infection rate, including the facts that mobile devices operate on private cellular networks; mobile operating systems are generally more secure than their PC counterparts; mobile device users do not usually have administrative control;

and mobile devices are newer, with better protection features built-in and automatically enabled.

However, a challenge for mobile devices is users can not simply click "update now" to ensure their mobile devices have the latest operating system patches and are configured securely. Mobile device operating systems are controlled by carriers, and may not get updates in a timely fashion. Older mobile devices that are no longer supported may not get updates at all. As a consequence, if mobile device operating systems are vulnerable and no longer being supported, then they are more susceptible to being "fundamentally more insecure" than PCs.

To address mobile operating system vulnerabilities for your smartphone or tablet, you should consider the following:

- **Know your operating system and version.** Know if you are running Google's Android or Apple's iOS operating system, and what version it is. Newer versions are generally more secure.
- **Make sure your operating system is up-to-date.** Go into your operating system and "check for updates." If an update is available, install it. If your operating system has not been updated lately, check with your carrier or device vendor to see if it is still being supported.
- **Use caution if it is no longer being supported.** If your device is no longer being supported, understand that it could be vulnerable. Use caution when you use it to surf the web, open e-mail, or install apps. Make sure the apps you install are from the official app stores and are reputable.
- **Consider retiring out-of-date devices.** If your device is no longer supported, consider retiring it for a more up-to-date device. Most likely it is getting a little slow to run the latest mobile games, anyway.

Addressing Smartphone or Tablet "Rooting"

One of the greatest security measures on mobile devices is the fact the user does not have "administrator" privileges, so all configuration changes are controlled and protected by the operating system. "Rooting" bypasses this protection by exploiting a flaw in the operating system to break the operating system's security and give the application complete control of the device. Another term for this is "jailbreaking" on iOS. Once you have rooted your device, you can change operating system parameters, install new versions of the operating system, change operating system icons, or replace the overall look and feel of the device.

Rooting is a very powerful tool in the hands of a skilled computer scientist, and developers may use rooting to install completely different operating systems on their devices, as well as to enable external peripherals. Once a device is rooted, it becomes much like a PC with endless expansion and customization possibilities. The problem is once a device has been rooted, applications can run with administrator privileges as well, and a malicious app can reconfigure the device at will. For many malicious apps, checking if the device has been rooted is the first thing they do after they have been installed. The most dangerous malicious apps will root your phone on their own, so they can take complete control of it.

To address the risks associated with rooting your smartphone or tablet, you should consider the following:

– **Do not root your primary device.** Understand that rooting makes your device extremely vulnerable. For your primary mobile device that contains your contacts, photos, messages, and passwords to be rooted is generally not a good idea.

– **Occasionally check that your device is not rooted.** Android and iOS app stores have applications that can tell you if your phone or mobile device has been rooted or jailbroken. Use them occasionally—perhaps a couple times a year—to make sure your primary device continues to be secure.

Reducing Smartphone or Tablet Malicious Apps Risk

Android and iOS phones and tablets come with the Google and Apple app stores built-in and are easily accessible. However, the app stores are not the only ways to install applications. There are alternative app stores, like the Amazon app store, and many app stores in China. Early Android tablets made extensive use of these alternative stores, because tablet manufacturers were not sanctioned by Google for use of the official app store.

Downloading apps from non-sanctioned app stores allows you to bypass the protection provided by the official stores. Google and Apple filter applications for malicious content, and while those filters are not perfect, they tend to work fairly well. In fact, the most malicious mobile applications frequently require bypassing the app stores, because they contain code for "rooting" your device or performing other activity that is not allowed by Google or Apple. However, this filtering also means some potentially useful applications are not available through the app stores. Filtering or not, it is entirely possible to install malicious applications onto your phone or tablet, and you must use caution.

To reduce the risk of malicious applications on your smartphone or tablet, you should consider the following:

- **Stick with the App Store.** You are always safest sticking with the app store, but malicious apps *do* sneak into these environments on an occasional basis. Malicious apps tend to masquerade as utilities, tools, gadgets, or free games.
- **Watch out for apps that are removed from the store.** If your favorite utility app has been removed from the store, it may have been malicious. Consider removing it from your smartphone or tablet, or at least researching its legitimacy and safety.
- **Use Mobile Security.** There is antivirus software available for mobile devices from mainstream vendors like Norton and Symantec. These tools tend to detect malicious apps faster than the stores might.
- **Watch out for excessive permissions.** Malicious apps tend to ask for permissions that are excessive and should be unnecessary. An emoji program does not need to access your camera or location. Beware of apps that ask for administrative privileges, or access to storage, keyboard, or location information that should be unnecessary. Deny the request and uninstall the app.
- **Watch out for rooting or battery drain.** Malicious apps may root your device or drain your battery running in the background. If you find your battery performance has deteriorated after installing an app that should not be running all the time, be concerned.
- **If in doubt, factory reset your device.** If you have installed a mobile app that rooted your device, your best bet is going to be to do a factory reset. You may not be able to successfully uninstall the malicious app.

Securing Bluetooth and Wi-Fi Networking

Mobile devices have a variety of wireless technologies built in, including cellular, Bluetooth, and Wi-Fi networking. Noncellular tablets still tend to include Bluetooth and Wi-Fi for local networking. Bluetooth networking is primarily used for connecting to peripherals like headphones, headsets, and personal computers. Wi-Fi networking is used to connect to home networks, high-speed internet, and also to create local cellular hotspots. While powerful, when these wireless networking technologies are enabled, others can see and potentially connect to your devices. Malicious users can use these connections to potentially exploit your devices, if they are vulnerable.

To securely use Bluetooth and Wi-Fi networking on your smartphone or tablet, you should consider the following:

- **Disable when not using.** When you are not using Bluetooth or Wi-Fi networking, you should disable them in the control panel. This precaution makes your device more secure, while also reducing battery drain.
- **Use trusted peripherals.** For your Bluetooth peripherals, use trusted devices from known vendors. Be concerned if your speaker wants to access your keyboard, or other weird behavior. If you encounter a malicious peripheral, stop using it and seek out a replacement from a more reputable vendor.
- **Configure a hotspot password.** If you use wireless hotspot features, make sure they are protected with a secure password. You do not want to operate an insecure hotspot that allows anyone to use your cellular data bandwidth.
- **Watch out for public Wi-Fi.** When you connect to a public Wi-Fi network, your device may be visible to everyone else at the same location. Be cautious at coffee shops, hotels, or conventions. Disable "automatic Wi-Fi connection" and only connect to public Wi-Fi when necessary.

Protecting Your Smartphone and Tablet Location Privacy

Perhaps a greater concern than wireless connectivity is location service. Many mobile devices include global positioning service (GPS) that allows them to calculate rapidly where on the planet you are, using satellite signals. While this capability does not generally work inside a building, once a device goes outside it can rapidly figure out where it is. This service is at least partially enabled all the time, so you can make an emergency call (using 911 in the United States) to request assistance. The emergency call automatically transmits your GPS coordinates to emergency responders, in case you are unable to tell them yourself.

Other services like Google Maps, Apple Maps, and Waze provide navigational services that automatically track your location and estimate traffic flows and density. This feature is sometimes called *location reporting*. In addition to these apps, your devices may record your location periodically during the day, and then store that information locally in a file. This feature is sometimes called *location history*. The problem with all of this location information is it means that your devices know where you are and may be reporting that information to others. Often, this location reporting is occurring without your knowledge or attention.

To configure location services to protect your privacy on your smartphone or tablet, you should consider the following:

- **Know big data is watching you.** Assume your device is tracking you and reporting your location to "big data," unless you have taken measures to turn such tracking off. If you're going someplace confidential, leave your phone at home or turn it off.

- **Check location reporting and history.** Go into settings on your phone and disable location reporting. You may also be able to do this on a control panel, but you should double-check in "settings" to be sure. Leave location reporting off unless you need to do navigation. You may also delete your location history this way, but it depends on your particular device.

- **Check application permissions.** Check your applications, as many of them may ask for location data but not need it to work properly. That stargazing app needs your location to show you the night sky, while that emoji app probably does not.

Using SMS-Based Messaging and Authentication Safely

Another powerful capability of smartphones is short message service (SMS) messaging, otherwise known as text messaging. With text messaging, we can quickly send short text messages to each other, and receive them from others. With more advanced multimedia messaging service (MMS) we can also send and receive pictures and videos to multiple recipients simultaneously. Some websites use SMS or MMS as an additional, multifactor, authentication method to allow us to use our phones to prove our identities, providing additional protection beyond username and password. Unfortunately, the protocols underlying SMS and MMS are not inherently secure, so it is relatively easy to "spoof" or send fraudulent SMS or MMS messages to recipients.

To safely use SMS-based messaging and authentication on your smartphone or tablet, you should consider the following:

- **Watch out for fraudulent texts.** Attackers may attempt to reach you via text message generated from their computer and appearing to be business-related or from friends or family. Do not respond to text messages from people you do not know or that were unsolicited, to avoid validating your phone number to potential scammers. Scammers who can validate your phone number may then follow up by trying to call you for personal information. Do not open links embedded in text messages, unless you know exactly what they are and who sent them.

- **Know how to send from e-mail to text.** Major cellular carriers have special e-mail services that allow you to send an e-mail to your phone number, and have it appear on your device as a text message. Find out if you have this capability for your carrier and send yourself a text, so you know what it looks like.
- **Use SMS authentication with caution.** SMS authentication is generally better than simple username/password authentication, but it is by no means foolproof. Attackers may attempt to intercept, spoof, or otherwise attack website multifactor authentication that uses text messaging. Determined attackers may even hijack your phone, just so they can get access to banking accounts protected by SMS. If large amounts of money are at stake, consider multifactor authentication methods that are stronger than SMS, like physical tokens or mobile authenticator apps.

Using BYOD and Mobile Device Management

Using your personal mobile device for work is called "bring your own device" or BYOD. It involves being able to access your enterprise e-mail, contacts, and other data from your personal mobile device. Enterprises like allowing this capability because it means they do not have to pay for mobile devices and cellular service for their employees. Employees like doing BYOD because it means they only have to carry around one device, and also because they may be able to get reimbursement for some or all of their mobile expenses. To do BYOD securely, enterprises may use mobile device management (MDM) technology.

MDM establishes a secure "bubble" on the mobile device, and keeps most enterprise data segregated within the bubble. Enterprise e-mail, contacts, documents, and web browsing may be conducted within the bubble. Data transferred using MDM is encrypted over the internet and authenticated to protect it from being intercepted. Data stored on the device using MDM is encrypted and stored in a secure area of the device. For additional security, MDM may establish a second password or PIN that you must enter to get into MDM-protected applications and data. MDM may also enable the enterprise to remotely "wipe" its data from your phone, or even erase your phone completely, should it be lost or stolen.

To use BYOD and MDM on your smartphone or tablet, you should consider the following:

- **Comply with your organizational policy.** To use BYOD and MDM, you are going to need to comply with your organizational policy regarding your personal mobile device. This policy may include establishing a strong PIN code on your device, turning on device storage encryption, or establishing additional device administrators.

- **Understand the impact of MDM.** In addition to subjecting your personal mobile device to an external policy, MDM may use up storage, resources, and battery on your device. Do not be surprised if your battery life is impaired due to the additional overhead of having MDM software constantly running on your device.

- **BYOD may not be for everyone.** If you are a senior executive, or if you operate a personal business on the side, mixing your personal mobile activity with your business mobile activity may not be a good idea. Also, if you have an older personal smartphone, the performance impact of MDM may simply be unacceptable.

- **Do not rule out getting a second device.** There are advantages to keeping your work life and home life separate. Using your personal cell phone for work may mean your personal phone number ends up on call lists for telemarketers and spam, which may be undesirable. If your personal life is complicated enough as it is, asking your employer to get you a second phone just for work may be a simpler approach.

Chapter 7
Protecting Your Web Browsing

For most of us, browsing the internet, or "surfing the world wide web," is one of the top uses for our personal computer, tablet, or smartphone. Whereas in the physical world, it is relatively easy to distinguish good neighborhoods from bad, in the virtual world different neighborhoods, businesses, and even countries are all just a click away from each other. It is easy to confuse www.organization.gov (a government organization site), www.organization.com (a private company site), and www.organization.org (a potential nonprofit site). And those sites are just a few examples. There are also websites ending in ".info," ".biz," and country code websites like ".us" for the United States and ".ru" for Russia, to name just two of more than two hundred.

When we surf the web, we do not know when we are going to end up in a bad neighborhood, or when our favorite website may turn against us through a malicious ad, a malicious link in a friend's posting, or a malicious e-mail. Search engines are amazing tools, but even innocuous searches can easily turn up content we would not want to share with our families. Safe web browsing involves avoiding the disreputable corners of the web, recognizing them when we stumble into them, and protecting ourselves when we find ourselves being attacked.

This chapter describes how you can use your computer to browse the web safely, and reduce risk to your computer, your data, and your privacy.

How the Web Works

To establish a presence on the internet, a person or business can do one of two things:
– Establish an identity online, like an *e-mail address* or a *personal web page*, using an established internet service like Facebook or Yahoo.
– Obtain a *domain name* and deploy a *web server* to display web pages that appear when people type that domain name into their web browser.

The first approach is free or inexpensive, while the second approach may require an investment ranging from a couple of dollars for a basic site to millions of dollars for a large, complex website able to support large numbers of users. In general, anyone can obtain any internet name they want, so long as it is available.

The end of the domain name is significant. It is called a top-level domain (TLD). The most common TLDs used in the United States are ".com,".org," and

DOI 10.1515/9781501506505-007

".gov," but there are over a thousand TLDs supporting infrastructure, business, nonprofits, and individual countries. Because of the large number of TLDs, it is difficult for legitimate organizations to control all possible versions of their names online. At the same time, it is relatively easy for attackers to register names similar to legitimate organization names. Attackers frequently use this similarity in names to trick internet users and take advantage of them.

When you type in the name of a website—like www.google.com—several things happen. First, your computer asks your network provider for an internet protocol address corresponding to www.google.com. This address is like a telephone number, and allows the computers to talk to one another. Once your computer has the address, it sends a request over the internet to the computers at Google, asking to see their website. Computers at Google then reply to your computer by sending the contents of the page. Similarly, when you click on links in an internet search result, your computer connects to other computers at other organizations to obtain the desired web pages.

Just as criminal elements in the physical world tend to set up shop in the shadows of the underworld, criminal elements set up shop on the internet as well. In practice, what has emerged over time are three distinct internets, all sharing the same global network and able to communicate with each other:
- *The reputable internet,* representing legitimate organizations and businesses intending to perform legitimate business, service, and commerce online.
- *The disreputable internet,* using the legitimate internet to conduct criminal and unethical activity, including fraud, theft, and extortion.
- *The dark web,* using internet technologies but operating hidden, private communities built to avoid infiltration by competing interests and the authorities.

The dark web is hidden from view and we are unlikely to stumble on it by accident, but a simple typo in the name of an e-commerce site can land you in the disreputable internet quite easily. In the next few sections we describe how the disreputable internet may target you and your computer.

Using Web Communication Protocols: HTTP versus HTTPS

Another important concept in how the web works is the concept of web security. In general, when you type the name of a site, or fill out a form on the web, the text you type is sent *in the clear* to the computer at the other end of the connection, and that computer's response is sent *in the clear* back to you. If you are typing in your username and password for your checking account, or the bank's website is sending you your checking account data, that information would be visible to everyone on the internet between your computer and the bank's computer. The protocol used for the "clear" connection, called hypertext transmission protocol (HTTP) does not inherently protect the information that is being transmitted.

Obviously, having your personal information transmitted over the internet in the clear so everyone can read it is not preferred. So, the internet designers extended the HTTP protocol to include security and called it the hypertext transmission protocol secure (HTTPS). When you type or see https:// at the beginning of a website name, you know the web browser is establishing a *secure* connection to the computer at the other end, and then using that secure connection to transmit and receive your information in a secure fashion.

To use web protocols for safe web browsing, you should consider the following:

- **Watch your browser bar.** At the top of your web browser window, there is an address bar that shows exactly where on the internet you are, and contains the web protocol, the DNS name for the site, and the specific page within the site. When you are using a secure connection, the address starts with https:// and you may also see the bar show a "physical lock" icon to the left or the right of the address. Under some circumstances, the bar may turn green to indicate a secure connection, or red to indicate an insecure connection (this indication depends on the browser and website).
- **Make sure your connection is secure.** If you are doing anything secure or private—including entering credentials, accessing personal information, or doing e-commerce—make sure your connection is secure. Today, most sites doing *anything* personal or sensitive use security, and you should expect it.
- **Do not enter passwords into insecure sites.** You should *never, never, never* be asked to enter a password into a site that is not using https:// protection! The only exception to this rule is small websites for your neighborhood or friends (although even they should be able to secure their login pages). If you think the site is okay based on conversations with your neighbors or friends, use a unique password that you do not mind getting compromised, and do not share that password with other websites.
- **Beware of certificate problems.** Occasionally, you may encounter a secure website that has a problem with its certificate. Your browser may give an error message saying that the website's security has a problem. This error can indicate a technical problem with a legitimate website, or it can indicate malfunctions associated with various types of cyberattacks. Avoid using sites when this problem occurs.

Avoiding Malicious Sites, Malvertising, and Pop-Ups

At the heart of web attacks are malicious websites and malvertising. Malicious websites are built and operated by attackers intending to attack computers that come to them. These sites may contain useful information, offer free software downloads, or be included in an e-mail campaign as a "recommended" destination for you to access. The key here is the sites are built and operated by the attackers. Some attackers operate campaigns that stand up and tear down dozens of websites a day, all fully automated. This automation allows attackers to stay ahead of authorities trying to shut their sites down.

Malvertising is somewhat more insidious than malicious websites because it involves creating malicious web advertisements and using the advertisements to attack viewers of legitimate sites. The problem here is when a web page includes advertisements, those advertisements are "mini web pages" embedded into a larger web page. They use the same technologies and capabilities to display the advertisement as a full web page, and so they can use the same techniques to attack the viewer as a malicious website. The most reputable advertisers—— like Google and Microsoft——go to great lengths to block such malvertising, but smaller advertisers are not so diligent and clever attackers may find workarounds to their protections.

In both cases, you may see malicious pop-up or pop-under windows. Pop-ups are when a website opens another web browser window over the top of the one you are currently looking at. Pop-unders are when a website opens another web browser window underneath the one currently open. In both cases, the new window has access to your computer to display material, play sounds, and possibly to access your peripherals like hard drives, cameras, and microphones. The most malicious pages create pop-ups that reappear every time you try to close them, forcing you to kill the program or reboot your computer to make the pop-ups go away. These windows often contain messages associated with some internet scam seeking to get your private information or payment.

Finally, attackers sometimes compromise legitimate websites and turn them to their use. There have been several cases of cyberattacks that compromised internet retailer sites and used the compromised sites to collect usernames, passwords, and credit card numbers. These attacks are usually conducted stealthily, so the site operators do not know they are compromised. As a user, you most likely only find out about the compromised retailer sites when the press reports the compromise, or if you see abuse of your accounts like invalid logons or fraudulent credit card charges.

To avoid malicious sites, malvertising, and pop-ups for safe web browsing, you should consider the following:

- **Use web security.** Many computer security antimalware packages also include web security features (these packages may also include family web filters such as parent controls). Enable these features to help you catch malicious sites and protect your computer from malicious attack or malvertising.
- **Know where you are on the internet.** As you browse the web, know where you are on the internet. It is very easy to start clicking on links and realize you are on web pages you have never heard of and never been to before. Stick with legitimate websites you know and trust and be cautious of links that take you to pages on other websites.
- **Watch out for typos and imposters.** Attackers frequently buy up web domains that are just one typo away from legitimate domains—like "www. microsft.com" (instead of www.microsoft.com), and then use that site for malicious purposes. The imposter site may look exactly like the legitimate site, to try to trick you into entering your credentials.
- **Do not search for free stuff.** Searching the internet for free copies of software, movies, music, or e-books is a good way to stumble into the disreputable internet. Sites hosting this pirated and copyrighted content know they are committing a crime, which means they probably do not mind hacking their visitors, either. Just like visiting "the bad part of town," the shadier your intentions are online, the more likely the websites you visit will be shady as well.
- **Be cautious of ads for products and services you have never heard of.** While lots of advertising serves useful purposes to educate potential customers, malicious ads are just "covers" for their true intentions. Malvertisers may advertise phony products they just made up to try to get you to click on their ad and go to their site.
- **Do not call technical support.** Malicious sites and pop-ups may tell you your computer has been infected or you have performed a crime, and you need to call immediately a technical support phone number. *Do not make the technical support call!* These numbers send you to call centers that specialize in compromising your computer and getting you to pay them fraudulent fees for help you do not actually need.
- **Avoid pop-up purgatory.** The worst pop-ups appear and then will not let you close them until you click a link within the page. *Do not click!* Instead, close the window from the operating system—in Windows, right-click in the taskbar and select close, or click "Ctrl, Alt, Delete" and use the Task Manager to close the window. If those approaches do not work, close out your other work and reboot your computer to make the pop-up window go away.

- **Watch out for pop-unders.** When a site creates a pop-under, you may see your screen flash before the window disappears. You may also see an additional window appear in your task bar or icon dock. When such activities occur, check them out and close them. Also, double-check where you are in your main window to make sure you have not stumbled onto a malicious site.
- **Watch out for installers.** The most dangerous sites try to install programs when you open the web page. They may masquerade this behavior, saying "we need to install a media player" or presenting other deceiving messages. Generally, no legitimate web page should need you to install additional software to view their page, unless the requirement is clearly marked and explained (such as for a special viewer or other unusual feature). If you see this behavior, stop what you are doing and double-check everything to be sure it is legitimate before you install.
- **Watch out for system administration.** Similarly, no website should require administrative privileges to show its content to you. If you are browsing the web and your operating system asks if you want to allow systems administration, *click "no" and immediately close your browser!* The site is most likely trying to hack your computer.
- **Some attacks may be persistent.** Some sites may succeed in installing software onto your computer or changing your home page, so their pop-ups continue even after you have closed all your browser windows and rebooted your computer. If this situation occurs, get professional help to remove the malware and clean up your system.

Using Web Browser Security and Plug-Ins

Your first line of defense when you stumble into the disreputable internet is your web browser. Web browsers may use "browser plug-ins" to enable additional functionality like the ability to click on a word and get its definition or to show a miniature version of a target web page when you hover over a link. There are a dizzying number of plug-ins available to enable all sorts of additional capabilities as you browse the web.

To use web browser security and plug-ins for safe web browsing, you should consider the following:
- **Choose a good browser for you.** All web browsers are not created equal and some browsers are more secure than others. For example, Internet Explorer on Windows may be needed for older websites with compatibility issues, but it has many known security vulnerabilities that do not make it suitable for

general web browsing. On the other hand, Google's Chrome browser works best with Google's accounts and online tools. Microsoft's "Edge" browser is built into Windows 10 and designed for speed and security, and Apple's "Safari" browser is built into iOS and MacOS devices. There are also open source web browsers like Firefox and Chromium. Weigh the tradeoffs and pick the right browser for the application—you may find yourself using multiple browsers, each best suited for a different purpose.

- **Make sure your browser is up-to-date.** Browsers are updated regularly to add functionality, fix bugs, and address security issues. *Make sure your browser is fully-patched before you go to a new website!* Patches may be through your operating system, through the browser, or automatic in the background. For example, Windows 10 automatically checks for patches and automatically downloads and installs the patches to keep the Edge and Internet Explorer browsers up-to-date. Other browsers usually have automatic update features—make sure they are enabled. If your browser has been recently updated, you may need to restart it to start using the latest version.

- **Watch your home page.** Another common attack vector is your home page. Sneaky attackers may change your home page to a counterfeit page that looks just like a legitimate home page like msn.com, yahoo.com, or google.com, but the counterfeit page is malicious. Make sure the home page looks right, that it uses web security (https), and that the address is correct (look for typos). If your home page is changed without your knowledge, it may be a sign your computer has been compromised.

- **Pay attention to plug-ins.** Plug-ins may also be called extensions or browsing helpers. Regardless, these tools can add significant functionality to your browser but are also a potential attack vector. Only install plug-ins you know, trust, and need, preferably obtained directly from the vendor. Occasionally check your plug-ins to make sure they are what you expect them to be. Remove plug-ins that are not expected or no longer needed, following the web browser documentation.

- **Make sure you are protected.** If your computer security software includes web filtering or website security, make sure the browser you are using is supported by that software (not all browsers may be). Most likely, the browser security is implemented using a plug-in from the computer security manufacturer. Make sure it is installed and enabled.

Protecting Your Browsing History

Remember that your browser knows where you have been! Web browsers maintain files and databases where they remember every page you visit and when you visited them. While this browsing history can be useful when you want to go back to a page you visited days or weeks ago, it also means your computer has a record of everywhere you have been and everything you have done. This history may be concerning, from a privacy perspective.

To protect your web browsing history for safe web browsing, you should consider the following:

- **Check your browsing history.** Occasionally, you should go into your browser and check your browsing history. If you see signs of visits to sites you have never heard of, or sites that may be malicious, then your browser or computer may have been compromised. Of course, another possibility is that another person has been using your computer.
- **Clear your browsing history and cache.** When your privacy is a concern, go into your browser and clear your browsing history. You should also clear your browser's cache. The cache is a storage area on your computer where the browser keeps temporary copies of websites and page data, so sites can download faster the next time you visit them. Instructions on how to clear the browser's history and cache are easily found online.
- **Watch out for kiosks.** Kiosk computers may keep the browsing history of every person who has used the kiosk, and you may or may not be able to clear the history when you are at the computer. If you can, clear your browser history and restart the computer after you use it, or at least logout of the kiosk service.
- **Remember bookmarks.** In addition to your browsing history, you can bookmark websites that you like for easy return. If you are concerned about your privacy, check your bookmarks and bookmarks that are sensitive or inappropriate.
- **Your history in the cloud.** Finally, remember many things you do online, particularly web searches, are stored in the cloud and may be directly associated with your online identity. For maximum privacy, go online and clear your history there, as well. Instructions for doing this are available from your search provider or cloud service.

Downloading Software Safely

While setting up your computer, you may find yourself going to websites to download and install software. Such software can include office productivity, utilities, and games. Software may come from manufacturer sites like microsoft.com or apple.com, software stores like amazon.com, or "freeware" software repositories like cnet.com. When you download and install software, you open the possibility of completely compromising your computer. Software installation frequently requires bypassing many of the computer's security mechanisms like administrator permissions and web firewalls. It involves bringing new code in from the internet and making that code able to run on your computer, pretty much at any time.

To download software safely from the web, you should consider the following:
- **Get software from legitimate sources.** Make sure the software you are downloading is from a legitimate source. For example, if you are downloading a software driver, make sure you are getting it from the manufacturer's website. Avoid driver "compatibility" sites that purport to scan your computer and find "missing" drivers, as these are often malicious. If you are downloading a game, make sure you are getting it from the game maker's website, not a copycat or imitation site. Where possible, get your software from "app stores" like the Microsoft or Apple stores, or your Linux distributor's online repository.
- **Watch out for "repackaged" software.** Attackers may download or pirate software, attach malware to it, and then repost it to software repositories. The resulting software will install properly and run properly, but unbeknownst to you the attached malware compromised your computer while it was installing. This situation is especially common with pirated versions of commercial software that should have been purchased in the first place.
- **Use antimalware scanning.** Make sure your antimalware software is installed and running when you download and install software from the internet. Some antimalware packages will scan installation files for malware before you install them, either automatically, or by right-clicking on the install file. Use these features if you have them available.

Chapter 8
Protecting Your E-Mail and Phone Calls

After web browsing, e-mail is probably the next most common use most of us have for our computers, especially at work. But e-mail can be a power for malice, as well as for good. Just as our coworkers and friends use e-mail to easily stay in touch with us, attackers can use e-mail to get to us as well. In fact, most enterprises consider e-mail to be the most common and dangerous technique attackers use to conduct cyberattacks.

In addition to being a path for attackers to target us, our e-mail accounts may also be the cornerstone of our online identities, as well. Websites use e-mail to notify us of account expirations, renewals, password changes, suspicious activity, and e-commerce transactions. Frequently, we use e-mail messages to prove to websites that we are who we say we are. So, our e-mail accounts need to stay safe, secure, and under our control. In addition to e-mail, we may also be targeted by telephone for various scams, or to attempt to take control of account password reset mechanisms.

This chapter discusses security for your communications, and includes how to protect your e-mail accounts, how attackers target you via e-mail, and how you can protect yourself against e-mail and other communications that may be malicious.

How E-Mail Works

The simple mail transfer protocol (SMTP) allows computers to communicate with one another by exchanging store-and-forward messages. Store-and-forward means that when you send an e-mail, it may not get to its destination immediately, but it will get there eventually.

To use e-mail, you must have an e-mail address and a mailbox. The e-mail address uniquely identifies you on the internet, just like a web address identifies a website. The e-mail address is formatted as "username@domain" where username is a unique user name, and domain is a DNS (domain name system) name, just like a web address. Your company website and your e-mail address use the same DNS, so the domain names are usually the same. Your e-mail mailbox resides on a server that is usually always running and connected to the internet. By having the mailbox always running, you can always receive e-mail, even when you are not actively connected or sitting at your computer. There are two primary approaches for setting up an e-mail account:

DOI 10.1515/9781501506505-008

- Create an e-mail account at an established internet service like Gmail or Yahoo, and use their mailbox service. This approach gives you an e-mail address yourname@gmail.com or yourname@yahoo.com that ends with the domain name of the service you are using.
- Establish your own mailbox service on a mail server you operate, which enables you to create any e-mail addresses you want, including multiple e-mail addresses. These e-mail addresses can include name1@yourdomain, name2@yourdomain, name127@yourdomain, and anything and everything in between.

The first approach is typically free or inexpensive, while the second approach requires that you establish your own mailbox server and infrastructure, like with hosting your own website. With both approaches, you get an e-mail address you can use on the internet. Registering for more than one e-mail address, or even hundreds or thousands of e-mail addresses, is relatively straightforward.

In addition to the ease of obtaining your own e-mail addresses, there is a second challenge to consider. The SMTP protocol specification does not include any built-in security. Consequently, it is possible for any computer to connect to any other computer speaking the SMTP protocol and send any e-mail message it wishes to that computer. E-mail protocols have been updated in recent years to include protection against potential malicious, counterfeit, or illegal e-mails. However, such protections are not 100% complete. Due to gaps in the security and its implementation, it is possible that the e-mails you get may not be what they appear to be.

Preventing Unauthorized Access to Your E-Mail Account

A first line of defense in protecting your e-mail has to do with access to your e-mail account. For web-based e-mail like Gmail, Microsoft Hotmail, or web services like Yahoo, the e-mail account is primarily protected by knowledge of your e-mail address (or username) and a password associated with the account. Multifactor authentication may also be available for your e-mail account. The use of multifactor technology for personal e-mail accounts is still relatively uncommon, while it is more commonly used for corporate e-mail accounts.

A major problem with e-mail is that people frequently use it to reset passwords for other accounts when those passwords have been lost or stolen. So, if an attacker gets control of your e-mail account, they may then be able to go to other accounts you use—like your online social media, gaming, shopping, or banking accounts—and then click on "forgot my password" to request an e-mail to allow them to reset the password. This technique works even if you have created separate, high-security passwords for your other accounts. Also, because attackers have access to your e-mail account, they can also delete the e-mail messages indicating that your account password was reset. In this way, they can cover their tracks and leave you in the dark that you have been hacked.

To prevent unauthorized access to your e-mail account, you should do the following:

- **Use good password practices.** Consider the guidance in "Chapter 4: Protecting Your Passwords" about creating and maintaining strong passwords and rotating them regularly. When you access your e-mail from untrusted devices like friends' computers, coworkers' computers, or kiosk computers, you should assume the computer is compromised and everything you are doing is being recorded. Access as few accounts as possible and change your passwords afterward from a trusted computer or device.
- **Turn on multifactor authentication.** If possible, enable multifactor authentication, which requires that you use a trusted computer to access your e-mail, or that you authorize access from a trusted device like your cell phone or your home phone. Note that multifactor authentication may not be compatible with older versions of e-mail clients like Microsoft Outlook, Android, or MacOS. You may have to do some testing to make sure everything works acceptably well.
- **Check the password reset mechanism.** Attackers who want access to your e-mail may try to get in through the password reset mechanism. Since your e-mail account can not send a password reset message to itself, this situation means there will be a dependency on *another* e-mail account, or a mobile device or telephone. Set up your e-mail password reset so it does not make your account more vulnerable to attack. If you have multiple e-mail accounts, configure them to back each other up, or to depend on access to a trusted telephone number. Make sure all these mechanisms are protected by different strong passwords!
- **Watch for unauthorized logins.** In some e-mail clients like Gmail and Hotmail, you can check your account for login activity and recent security events like password resets. Use these tools periodically—maybe once a month—to make sure your accounts remain secure. Some tools can even tell you where in the world access attempts came from.
- **Watch your junk and deleted e-mail folders.** Depending upon your e-mail application, malicious e-mails may get automatically detected and routed to your junk mail folder. Also, when attackers attempt to cover up their tracks, they may accidentally leave messages in your deleted e-mail folder. Periodi-

cally check both folders for suspicious activity. In your junk e-mail folder, you want to watch for e-mails that appear to be legitimate or appear to be from businesses you use or people you know. Such e-mails may indicate the businesses or people have been compromised or are being used to target you with phishing or spear phishing attacks. In your deleted e-mail folder, look for messages you did not delete. If those messages are related to password resets, account access, or logins to your accounts, you may have a problem. You should access your accounts to check for unauthorized transactions, password resets, or other activities you do not recognize. Contact your account holders (e.g., bank, credit card company) and inquire about such activities and reset your account accesses with strong passwords.

– **Check your account.** As previously mentioned, the website www.haveibeen-pwned.com checks your e-mail account against a number of publicly available databases to see if there are signs that account has been compromised or its password may have been made available to hackers. This functionality is so useful that it has been integrated into the Firefox web browser. If you find evidence your account has been *pwned* (this means your *password* has been *owned*, hence *pwned*) make sure you change your password immediately and keep a vigilant eye on all your accounts for possible malicious behavior.

– **Be prepared to reset your account.** If you find a sign that one of your e-mail accounts has been compromised or is under active attack, be prepared to reset your account. Resetting your account involves the following actions:
   o   Make sure you can logon to the account.
   o   Change your password.
   o   Update the password on all your devices and any password managers you use.
   o   Make sure the updated password is not used on any of your other accounts, and if so update them as well.
   o   Double-check your password reset mechanism and its dependencies.
   o   Keep a vigilant eye on all your accounts and activity for 30–90 days.

Recognizing Malicious E-Mail

In addition to trying to take over your e-mail account, attackers may try to send you malicious e-mails. Malicious e-mail messages are by far the most common avenue for attackers to target victims and their computers. Malicious e-mails generally target computers in one of the following ways:

E-mail display attack. When the user views a malicious e-mail, the e-mail exploits a vulnerability in the e-mail viewer or the operating system to take control of the victim's computer. These attacks are only occasionally possible—e-mail viewer security is generally quite good—although there have been a few documented cases where e-mail display attack campaigns have been successful.

Malicious attachment attack. Attached to the e-mail, there are documents intended to trick the user or compromise their computer or device. These attachments may be actual software programs (uncommon), documents containing malicious content (more common), or documents that link to malicious websites (very common).

Malicious link attack. Within the e-mail, there are links to malicious websites that attempt to compromise the victim's computer, trick the victim into entering credentials, or trick them into installing software that compromises their accounts or devices. This approach is also quite common.

Due to protections put in place by e-mail client vendors, and users becoming more cautious about attached documents and programs, malicious links and attachments have become the most common techniques used by malicious e-mail messages. E-mail solicitations have exploded, but are also increasingly filtered out by e-mail systems. Malicious e-mail attackers continue to adapt their techniques to get past the lines of defense and into your inbox.

To recognize potentially malicious e-mails, you should do the following:
- **Watch out for unexpected offers.** The first sign of potentially malicious e-mails are e-mails that are unexpected, or present offers that are "too good to be true." E-mails might say you need to click on a link to get money, or the attachment contains an invoice you need to read, or you need to install a program to safeguard your computer. If you were not expecting an e-mail notification or did not expect to get an e-mail with a document attached to it, the e-mail may be fraudulent.
- **E-mails telling you to act urgently.** Another theme of malicious e-mails is they usually contain some pressure to act. Attackers may have to move quickly to stay ahead of authorities (and antimalware). If an e-mail is telling you to act now, resist the temptation and wait a bit.
- **E-mails claiming to be an authority.** Malicious e-mails frequently claim to be an authority or other legitimate organization. They may claim to be from the IRS, the FBI, the police, a bank, a store, or a shipper. A particularly effective technique is to tell people they have a package and need to click on a link

to arrange delivery. While an offer of money is usually too good to be true, what if you really *did* receive a package? Shippers usually have other ways to legitimately contact you, or to let you know the status of your shipment.

- **Links to unexpected places.** Links in malicious e-mails seldom go to legitimate destinations. Hover over links without clicking on them to make sure they are what they appear to be. For example, a link from your bank should point to the bank's website and not some other site. If you get an e-mail from fred@a1.com that contains a link to www.a1.com and you have never heard of "a1.com" then it may well be fraudulent. If you get an e-mail claiming to be from someone@fbi.gov but then the link points to www.a1.com you have even more reason to be suspicious. Hover over links and look at the web address. If the link does not start with a legitimate website that matches the e-mail address of the sender and is from an organization with which you do business, it is likely fraudulent.

- **Disguised attachments.** Another trick attackers use is to disguise malicious attachments as innocent-sounding documents. One way to disguise attachments is to give the documents names that include an extension for an Adobe PDF document, word processing document, or spreadsheet, but have an executable extension. Executable extensions include JavaScript (.JS), AppleScript (.SCPT) batch files (.BAT), command files (.COM), and program executables (.EXE). Depending on the configuration of your computer, you may not see the filename extension for the executable, but you may see that the icon for the document is not a document icon. Save attachments to your hard drive to examine them make sure they are what they appear to be. Documents should appear to be documents, not programs. At this point, you can also have your antimalware software scan the document, if such a feature is available. To open the document, open up the appropriate application and use it to open the document, rather than "double-clicking" to open the document from the operating system. Legitimate documents should not request to install anything when they are opened.

- **Application attachments.** A favorite attack technique is to get the victim to simply install malware. Even if the attachment is obviously a program, a small percentage of victims will install it. Attackers know they can e-mail a million users and still get thousands of "hits." Be very, very, cautious when you are directed to install software by some sort of online message. There is almost *no* legitimate reason why someone should e-mail you a program, unsolicited. Do not install or run application attachments unless you know exactly where they came from and why they had to be sent via e-mail. If you need to install software, it is much better to go to the vendor's website or the app store and install the software from there.

- **Unusual e-mails from people you know.** Phishing and spear phishing involve sending you e-mails that have been crafted to sound legitimate, and appear to be from people whom you know. Such "legitimate" e-mails are designed to increase the chances of you clicking on links, giving up your credentials, or installing malware. Spear phishing attacks use internet databases to target you personally, either from your personal address book, your social media contacts, or from other people with whom you have connections. Attackers may send e-mail using your name, your friends' or acquaintances' names, or even appearing to be from their e-mail addresses as well. If a message does not make sense, attempt to contact the sender using some other method—like a phone call—to see if it is legitimate.
- **Application install prompts.** When reading e-mail, you should be reading messages, opening documents, and going to websites. You are *not* installing software! If a software installation prompt pops up while you are reading your e-mail, you have likely stumbled into something malicious. Stop what you are doing, click "cancel," and do not proceed further. At work, you should report the suspicious e-mail to your internal computer support personnel and follow their instructions. At home, if you are using Microsoft Outlook, you should move the suspicious e-mail to your Junk E-mail folder, block the e-mail, empty the Junk E-mail folder, and then empty the Deleted Items folder. Alternatively, you can delete the suspicious e-mail and then empty the Deleted Items folder.

Recognizing Phishing, Spear Phishing, and Online Scams

Experts estimate that over a million new phishing websites are created every month, with many of those websites having a lifetime of less than 24 hours. Why is this? Because phishing is, by far, the most effective way for attackers to reliably get into target enterprises. Even if only 1% of people "click on the link" or "open the attachment," attacks that send millions of e-mails generate thousands of victims for the orchestrators. Attackers intent on getting into a target organization are almost guaranteed a foothold if they can send phishing e-mails to a large enough number of employees.

A little bit of terminology. Phishing e-mails are e-mails sent to victims and prompting them to do something. These e-mails have a goal of getting the victim to go to a malicious website, give up their personal information, enter their credentials, or install malware on their computer. Spear phishing e-mails have the same objective but are personalized to target specific individuals using databases of personal information. Online scams may include combinations of phishing, websites, and even telephone calls that are all orchestrated "as a system" to work together, usually to get money from the victim. In addition to these terms, there is "clone phishing" which involves manipulating copies of legitimate e-mails to make them malicious, and "whaling" which involves spear phishing targeted at senior executives or highly privileged users.

To recognize phishing, spear phishing, and online scams, you should watch out for the following:

– **Typos.** While e-mail attacks continue to get more sophisticated, their creators are only human, frequently in a hurry, and are often language-challenged. Typos, misspellings, and awkward phrasing are signs the e-mail message is phishing, rather than a legitimate message.

– **Nonspecific greetings.** Nontargeted phishing may use a nonspecific greeting for a message (e.g., To Whom it May Concern). When FedEx is telling you that you have a package, FedEx frequently structures the message so it greets you, includes particulars of your message, and other details so you can accurately understand the situation and what they need of you. Phishers doing a bulk mailing have none of these message elements, so the messages may be generic and nonspecific in an unusual way.

– **Inconsistent e-mail addresses.** While it is technically possible to create phony e-mails from legitimate domains (known as "spoofing" e-mail addresses), recent security improvements have made such spoofing significantly more difficult, especially for large companies with hardened information technology (IT) infrastructures. So, attackers simply send e-mails from the e-mail domains they do have, knowing this approach only reduces their attack success a little bit. For example, when you get an e-mail claiming to be from FedEx, but it does not originate from an "@fedex.com" e-mail address, be very suspicious.

– **Other recipients.** If the e-mail is sent to multiple recipients, are the other recipients people you would expect to see on the e-mail thread? Or is it a message that should be part of a thread that is only addressed to you? Attackers may use blind copy features to send a single e-mail to large numbers of recipients anonymously, but it means the e-mail to you looks more like a bulk e-mailing than a personal message. Unusual recipient lists can indicate a phishing attempt targeting your group or organization.

– **Unusual subject lines.** When we correspond legitimately, we tend to use subject lines that are specific to the issue, or reflect the conversation we are having. Similarly, a service notification usually reflects the service involved, or the issue. Phishing subject lines are frequently generic, or inconsistent with the other content of the message.

- **Links to fraudulent logon pages.** Another popular attacker technique is to tell you that you need to logon to an account to handle a problem, and then include a link to a page that looks just like the logon page for the account in question. It is relatively easy for attackers to copy the logon pages of banks, social media, or e-commerce sites, and make their counterfeit sites look just like the real things. Stop and take a hard look at the web address. Usually, the web address is completely wrong. If so, do not enter your credentials!
- **Asks for personal information.** Another attacker technique is to send you to a web page and then ask you for personal information like home address, telephone number, credit card number, or social security number. Some people enter the information just because they were asked for it. You should not need to enter your banking information to participate in a survey. For example, a survey that offers to give you money if you enter your banking information is probably "too good to be true" (see below).
- **Threats of penalties.** Attackers want you to act. They know their e-mail is going to get buried in your inbox in a matter of hours. Also, they frequently stand up and tear down their supporting infrastructure quickly —perhaps in a day or less. Therefore, they may include the threat of penalties in their e-mail message to prompt you to act quickly or immediately, while their entire scam is in place and ready to exploit you.
- **Offers too good to be true.** Another attacker technique is to give you an attractive offer. Attackers may say you owe money, but people are more likely to respond if they think they are *owed* money. Many of us have received offers to save hundreds of dollars on a cruise by booking now. There is a fine line between an offer that is a good deal versus one that is simply ridiculous. If you can not imagine a real business making the offer, it probably is not legitimate.
- **Technical problems, legal trouble, or package deliveries.** Common scams use threats of technical problems, legal troubles, or promises of package deliveries to try to get victims to click on a link or call scam phone numbers. Microsoft or Apple are not going to e-mail you to tell you your computer needs to be updated or that it has malware on it. Similarly, the FBI or IRS are not going to send you an e-mail saying you broke the law. While FedEx might e-mail you about a package delivery, you need to ask yourself if you were expecting a package in the first place, and then look up the tracking number on fedex.com to see if it is legitimate.
- **Current events.** Finally, some of the more sophisticated scams capitalize on current events. For example, after a natural disaster, there is an increase in scams pretending to be from the Red Cross or purporting to be crisis relief. At tax time, there is a significant increase in scams purporting to be from the IRS or alleging to be about your tax return. When U.S. Medicare announced

new ID cards in 2017, identity theft scams sent e-mails designed to exploit the transition, and spoofing the Medicare website to get seniors to give up personal information.

Guarding Against Counterfeit E-Mails and Secure E-Mail

Because e-mail protocols are inherently insecure, it may be possible for attackers to generate and send counterfeit e-mails. Counterfeit e-mails may appear to be from businesses where you have relationships, the government, or your friends. To reduce this risk, standards organizations have developed e-mail protections that make it harder to generate or transmit counterfeit e-mails. These protections include the sender policy framework (SPF), domain key identified mail (DKIM), and domain-based message authentication, reporting, and conformance (DMARC). These protections make it harder for attackers to counterfeit e-mails targeting protected organizations. However, these protections are not complete internet-wide, so one can not be guaranteed that any given organization is protected, all the time.

Consequently, you must be aware that counterfeit e-mails are always a possibility. This means an e-mail can still be malicious even if it appears to come from a legitimate organization where you have a relationship. The malicious e-mail can have a matching organization name and e-mail address. Further confusion comes from the fact that many legitimate e-mail messages come from third-party services providing payroll, shipping, facilities management, or other supporting business services.

To reduce these risks for the most sensitive e-mail messages, secure e-mail technologies are available for businesses to use. These technologies include the secure multipurpose internet mail extension (S/MIME) and pretty good privacy (PGP) standards, as well as web services for secure messaging. S/MIME and PGP messages may appear in your e-mail reader with lock or signature icons to show the messages are secure. Secure messaging web services, on the other hand, send you a text e-mail message that contains a web link to retrieve the actual message from a secure website. This technique is increasingly being used in the human resources and healthcare industries for sending sensitive personal information.

To guard against counterfeit e-mails and use secure e-mail, you should consider the following:
– **Be cautious.** Understand that counterfeiting technology enables attackers to spoof even legitimate e-mail addresses. So, you must recognize the message

is malicious based on other factors, like the context, the message, or suspicious links or attachments.

- **Know when secure messages are coming.** Customer service personnel are generally trained to tell you when to expect a secure e-mail using a secure web services. The challenge with these web services is that their messages include links you must click to get to the messages, which makes the messages look somewhat like phishing. Look at the messages carefully to make sure that everything is in order before you click the link. Secure messaging is usually used only for non-routine, confidential messages, rather than general business notifications.

- **Understand what S/MIME and PGP e-mail looks like.** Understand if your e-mail client can support secure e-mail, and what S/MIME or PGP messages look like in your e-mail client when you receive them. Unfortunately, not all e-mail clients can send or receive S/MIME or PGP messages, or require special software be installed beforehand. This limitation has hindered the adoption of these technologies.

- **Be careful of attachments and links.** Even with secure messages, watch out for attachments and links. Attachments should match the context of the message and should almost never include executable files. Examine links carefully to make sure they are sending you somewhere that makes sense and looks like the right place once you get there. If the link is to a secure message service like "zixmail" make sure the link matches the secure messaging provider's website or web service. If in doubt, open up a browser window and visit the secure e-mail provider's website to make sure.

Guarding Against Unsolicited Phone Calls

We all dislike getting phone calls from telemarketers or other unsolicited requests. "Robocall" technology can call a number, recognize if it gets an answering machine, and then even start a conversation with the person who answers the phone. Due to the rise of robocall technology and declining costs, the percentage of phone calls that are unsolicited is dramatically increasing each year. Some experts predict that in the future more than half the calls you receive on your cell phone will be robocalls. Due to gaps in telephone security, robocallers can also spoof telephone numbers to make the calls appear to come from someone in your area code or an organization with which you do business. Some of the more nefarious scams may try to get you to say phrases like "okay" or "yes" or "I want this" over the phone, so they can record your voice, impersonate you, and make fraudulent telephone transactions elsewhere on your behalf.

To guard against unsolicited phone calls and telephone-based fraud, you should consider the following:

- **Check with your phone company.** Some phone companies have services to automatically screen for unwanted, unsolicited, and potentially malicious scam calls. Inquire if this service is available for you, and activate it if possible.

- **Use the National Do Not Call Registry.** Register your home and mobile phone numbers with the National Do Not Call Registry, available at www.donotcall.gov. You can also report unwanted calls at this website.

- **Buy a call blocker.** Call blockers are devices that connect to your phone line and can filter which calls should be allowed through and which should be rejected. Some call blockers are manually configured, while others can automatically configure themselves, much like antivirus software on your computer. Configured call blockers can block robocalls, political calls, scam calls, and other unwanted calls.

- **Screen your calls.** If you have doubts about an incoming call, let it roll over to voicemail. If the call is legitimate, the caller will leave a message. If it is a telemarketer, robocall, or a scam of some sort, most likely the "caller" will not leave a message.

- **Be careful what you say.** Scammers may be trying to get you to say certain things so they can record and reuse your voice in a different context. If they ask, "can you hear me okay," or "are you the homeowner," simply respond with "why are you calling?" or "okay." Try not to say "yes," or "no," as recordings of you saying these words can be useful for fraud. Once you start questioning them, scammers will frequently hang up.

- **Watch for scam charges.** Watch your phone bills, credit card, and banking statements, especially after you have conducted business over the phone that seemed suspicious after-the-fact. If unauthorized charges are present, dispute them—the sooner the better.

Chapter 9
Protecting Your Identity, Privacy, and Family Online

With the rise of the internet, more and more of our personal lives reside in our computers, mobile devices, and online accounts. Yet, it is still important that our identities, privacy, and families be protected, even when they are all online and internet-connected. There is no one way to provide online privacy and security, so we need to be constantly vigilant.

This chapter discusses how we can protect our identity, privacy, and family online, while taking advantage of the power of having a digital life.

Controlling Your Anonymity Online

The internet and smartphones have led to an ever-accelerating change in how we approach personal liberty and anonymity. An example of this lack of privacy occurs when you look up something online—say a new car—and then go to your favorite news site. At the news site, you may see an advertisement for the car you were just looking at. In a matter of seconds, your search provider connected your search for cars in one screen, to an advertisement it is displaying on an information website in a completely separate browser window and maybe even on a completely separate device. Connecting your online searching to businesses wishing to sell to you is that fast, and disturbingly effective.

The reality here is organizations use "big data" analytics to monitor, capture, store, and analyze everything we do online. When we go to a website or send an e-mail, our computer is uniquely identified by its internet protocol (IP) address online. If we do a web search while logged in to our Microsoft, Google, Apple, or other online account, not only do these organizations capture the address of our computer, but they also capture our individual identity as well. The reason web searching is free—it costs millions to operate a search engine—is because the search providers count on advertising and data processing revenue to offset those costs. They not only use your searches to display "relevant" advertisements paid for by advertisers, but they also collect profiles on you based on your aggregate behavior and sell that information as well. The more you do online, the larger and more comprehensive your profiles are, and the more valuable those profiles are to businesses wishing to analyze them, or use them to sell to *you*.

DOI 10.1515/9781501506505-009

Consequently, it is almost impossible to be anonymous on the internet. While it feels like no one can see you surfing the web in a dark room at midnight, the fact is your computer, your web browser, your online accounts, your network provider, and the sites you visit, are all recording *everything* you do, and retaining that data for later analysis. While it is theoretically possible to be anonymous while using the internet, it is very difficult to do so in practice. As the prominent security technologist Bruce Schneier famously said, "if something is free, you are not the customer, you are the product."

Some things you can do to control your anonymity online include the following:

- **Be aware of national laws.** The European Union (EU) General Data Protection Regulation (GDPR) provides significant privacy protection for EU citizens, including the option for citizens to tell companies to "forget me" and delete all of those citizens' data. The United States does not have such regulations currently, although some U.S. states are considering enacting similar regulations. In some countries, the government is actively monitoring its citizens online, including the activity of visitors to those countries. Be aware of the online protections in your country, and other countries when you travel abroad.

- **Consider your internet service provider (ISP).** ISPs can see what websites you go to and can also see your interactions with those sites if the connections are unencrypted. When you use your smartphone to surf the web, your cellular provider is acting as your ISP, unless you are using a home Wi-Fi connection. To be anonymous, you would need to use a virtual private network (VPN) to connect to an anonymous networking service that obscures your online identity. Your ISP would know that you were connected to the VPN service and how much data you were sending or receiving, but not what you were actually doing.

- **Consider your web browser.** Just as your ISP sees everything you do; your web browser sees everything you do regardless of your ISP. Some browsers—like Google and Microsoft—allow you to logon with your account, and synchronize all your browsing data, passwords, and history across all of your devices. While this capability is great, it also means all that information is now being stored "in the cloud." Some browsers, like the "TOR Browser" include features to enable web browsing that is at least somewhat anonymous. With a regular browser, you can reduce the amount of data being stored by periodically clearing your browser's history, cookies, and cached passwords. For example, you can clear your Microsoft Edge browser data each time you close the browser by turning on one of the "Settings" features. However, this process is cumbersome.

- **Watch out for your applications.** The applications you use remember when you start the application, when you shut it down, and everything you do in between. If you filled out a product registration form when you installed the application, it knows who you are and where you live. Many major applications record this information and send it back to the vendor every time you run the application. While this information is allegedly for diagnostic purposes, it also means the vendor knows who you are and how you use their software.

- **Beware of e-commerce.** As soon as you purchase something online, the vendor knows who you are, where you live, and your credit card information. The vendor can also tie that information to your computer IP address and your account information, if you have an account with them. If you use a service like PayPal or Amazon, they have a record of this transaction along with all your prior transactions and can use them all to build profiles about you and your preferences.

- **Watch out for cookies.** Websites track users using "cookies" that are written to the user's computer's storage and presented back to the website each time the user returns. Cookies perform an important function to enable session tracking like when you are doing a transaction online. However, "persistent" cookies enable the site to recognize you every time you come back and link that information to your identity. All you had to do was identify yourself to them one time. Once the initial identification was performed, the cookie enables the site to recognize you and your devices, every time you visit.

- **Test your privacy.** The Electronic Frontier Foundation (EFF) is a nonprofit organization actively promoting online privacy causes. They have created several tools and services for protecting your privacy online, at www.eff.org. One of the more intriguing tools they have is the "panopticlick" service available at https://panopticlick.eff.org. You can use it to test your web browser's privacy configuration, against their standards. After testing your configuration, you may find you want to change your configuration, or install a privacy filter.

- **Do some research!** The above list is just a starting point for protecting your privacy online, as well as that of your family. Features like location tracking, notifications, file sharing, e-mail, and free software all give big data opportunities to track you and monetize your online activity. Consider everything you do, the devices you use, and the available tools to give yourself the levels of protection you think you need.

Protecting Your Family Online

Kids today will never know a life that is nondigital. Five-year-old kids know how to look up their favorite videos, and ten-year-old kids can not go a week without some kind of online social or game-playing experience. All this connectivity comes with risks. Just as kids are only one click away from their favorite online destinations, they are also just one click away from content and relationships that are inappropriate, offensive, or worse, dangerous. As parents, we want to enable our kids' online experiences, while also protecting their safety at the same time.

Some techniques you can use to protect your family online include the following:
- **Be aware of kids' online activities.** Pay attention to what your kids are doing online. Have open conversations with them about what they want to get out of the internet. Is it research for school? Videos for entertainment? E-mail or social media with friends? Online gaming? Understand what they are doing online, why, and where in the internet those activities take them. Explain to them how the internet is a dangerous place, and just as they need to be cautious with strangers in the real world, they need to be cautious online as well.
- **Configure their devices.** Kids almost *never* need administrative access to their devices. Installation of software and establishing accounts for them should be carefully supervised. If kids are surfing the web on the family computer, make sure they have separate accounts that are restricted in what they can do and where they can go. You do not want your kids getting malware on the family computer, or worse.
- **Put passwords on your other devices.** Kids are remarkable in their ability to figure things out, especially when a fun game, amusing video, or other gratification is involved. Identify which devices in your household are okay for kids to use, and which are not. Put passwords on all of them so you can control their usage, especially by young children.
- **Understand their online accounts.** Your kids will most likely need online accounts whether you like it or not. They may get accounts at school for online education, but those accounts may also be usable outside of school. They may need e-mail identities to receive license keys, may need to establish accounts with search engines to store their preferences, or may want accounts on gaming sites to play their favorite games. Keep a list of your children's online accounts, the websites where the accounts reside, and the passwords protecting the accounts.
- **Monitor their online connections.** More and more online sites and games include social media elements. It is hard to go to a website and not see a link to "connect through Facebook," "forward through Twitter," or "publish

to Instagram" on the site. Kids will want to connect with their friends online but can easily fall victim to connecting with strangers who show interest in them. Only let your kids connect to people they (and you) know in person. Periodically check their online connections to make sure you are up-to-date on who is interacting with your kids.

- **Use family protection technology.** Devices, operating systems, and application software are becoming more family-friendly aware. Microsoft and Apple both have family protection features built in to their operating systems that can be turned on to protect children. Also, popular internet security programs like Norton and Symantec include web filtering features that can be used to protect kids from inappropriate websites. These examples are but a few of the available options. Research these options, enable them, and monitor their operation.

- **Teach your kids about the internet.** As part of having open communications, educate your kids about how the internet works, its power and capabilities, and its dangers and risks. When they make mistakes, use those mistakes as teaching opportunities. Remember that you own the devices, and you can establish the rules for their use. Enforce your rules, even when the enforcement is unpleasant. Your kids will live, even if they are not online for hours every day, constantly connected to their favorite game, or active in their favorite social community.

Protecting Your Identity and Credit

In 2017 the credit rating agency Experian suffered a dramatic data breach that compromised the personal credit data of 143 million American consumers. According to Experian, the hackers "accessed people's names, social security numbers, birth dates, addresses, and possibly driver's license numbers." In addition, the hackers accessed credit card numbers for more than 200,000 people and credit dispute documents for about 180,000 people. This breach served as a wake-up call for the "data aggregation" business that collects data on millions of people but does not actually have direct relationships with those individuals. This industry includes credit rating agencies, credit card processors, advertisers, and thousands of other businesses in the business of collecting, processing, reporting, and selling data analysis services. It is a burgeoning industry.

To protect ourselves amid these breaches and compromises, we must protect our identities and credit in the physical world and online. This protection revolves around data. To protect your identity and credit ratings, you should consider the following:

– **Guard your documents.** There are several physical documents that serve as your identity "foundation." Armed with these documents, someone can attempt to impersonate you and steal your identity. These documents include birth certificates, social security cards, immigration documents, national passports, driver's licenses, Medicare cards, and national identification cards (in some countries). Have a minimum number of copies of these documents in your possession and safe deposit boxes or other secure storage, but do not make extra copies that could easily be lost or stolen. Any copies that are no longer needed should be thoroughly destroyed so they are completely illegible: shredding is okay, but burning is better.

– **Guard your identifying data.** In the United States, social security numbers have become *de facto* national identifiers, and it will take decades to reduce the danger of someone using your number to impersonate you. When accessing resources online or by telephone, your identity is just a matter of information data such as name, telephone numbers, home address, account numbers, e-mail addresses, usernames, and passwords. Your identity is confirmed using secondary identifying information, including: mother's maiden name, schools, favorite colors, pet names, and other personal trivia and preferences. Keep track of this information, and do not share it except when necessary.

– **Consider credit and identity monitoring.** Ironically, a big part of Experian's business is providing credit and identity monitoring. This service gives consumers control over the information the credit agency shares with their business customers and may allow the consumer to authorize when that information is shared. In addition, there are services like LifeLock that provide identity protection above and beyond the protection provided by the credit agencies. In addition, recent regulations in the United States have made it free to request a "credit freeze" that requires your authorization before credit is granted in your name. Credit agencies such as Experian, TransUnion, and Equifax provide "fraud alert" services that can provide similar protections in the event of identity theft.

– **Watch out for tax and medical identity theft.** Scams that involve stealing people's identities to obtain tax refunds, or to get free medical services, are becoming more common. Scammers may attempt to steal your identity to file false tax returns in your name and take the resulting refunds, before you can file legitimately. Medical fraud involves stealing your medical information and then getting medical services in your name or buying prescription drugs (which can then be re-sold for cash). These scams are disruptive, expensive, and time-consuming to address. Medicare recommends you guard your Medicare card like it is a credit card and only provide your Medicare number to people you know should have it. Like the IRS, Medicare does not call you unless you give them permission to contact you ahead of time. Review your Medicare claims for mistakes or suspicious charges, and report any irregularities to Medicare. To help prevent Medicare fraud and protect yourself, see https://www.medicare.gov/forms-help-resources/help-fight-medicare-fraud for more information.

- **Monitor your identity.** Where identity is concerned, a little paranoia can go a long way. Buy a shredder and shred identifying documents like monthly bills, credit card offers, account balances, and medical statements. In the United States, get your annual credit report from the major agencies—Equifax, Experian, and TransUnion—and check it carefully for personal information or accounts that are incorrect or not expected. Check your bank, credit card, and other statements carefully for fraudulent charges or unexpected transactions.

Safely Using E-Mail, Social Media, and Gaming

Outside of work, most of us have gotten used to "free" e-mail accounts from the likes of America Online, Yahoo, Hotmail, Microsoft, or Google. The same goes for social media services like Facebook, LinkedIn, Twitter, and Instagram. Of course, if it is free, it is also being monitored so the providers can make money from selling your information and behavior to advertisers, businesses, and data aggregators. All these services monitor your activity, postings, connections, and preferences, and are constantly inventing new ways to package and sell that data to whomever wants to buy it. They are also interested in selling access to you through your "network," knowing that products and services coming through your friends or network are more compelling than those simply presented by an advertiser.

To safely use e-mail, social media, and gaming online, you should consider the following:
- **The internet is forever.** Everything you post to the internet is going to be recorded, saved, backed up, archived, and made searchable by ever-increasing analytical engines. While you may not remember where in the internet you went last week, your web browser, search engine, and the sites you visited remember everything perfectly. *Assume that everything you post online*

is public and could appear on the front page of your favorite newspaper or news site, even decades from now.

- **Watch your e-mail.** Free e-mail is monitored and analyzed by the providers, who then sell that information to advertisers, aggregators, and other interested parties. They may also use your address book to establish connections between you and other people—your "web of connections." If you want real privacy, find an e-mail service that guarantees it, or operate your own e-mail server. It may cost money, but that may be a price worth paying if your privacy is that important to you.
- **Your "web of trust."** Do not be the friend who gets all their friends infected with malware, and do not fall victim if one of your friends is infected and tries to attack you. Be careful of the documents, links, and recommendations you make online. Be wary of what is recommended to you from your social network. Just because an e-mail or posting comes from a friend, does not mean the e-mail or posting is legitimate. Also, when you "like" something online you are establishing a connection to it and it can be used to get to you. Is it a connection that is safe? Is it a connection you want to endure long-term?
- **Safe social media.** Understand how your social media accounts interconnect with each other. Networking sites are all-too-happy to consume your address book and invite all your contacts to participate as well. Twitter is thrilled to broadcast to the world when you "like" a site on Facebook. Likes are often publicly accessible and can be used to profile you over time. Many of the major services have integrated together to make cross-sharing easy or even enabled by default. Look at your privacy settings, and make sure the appropriate amount of information is shared publicly, or with friends and family. You really do not need to share everything, especially with the public.
- **Watch whom you friend.** Be careful whom you "friend," especially when they are only acquaintances, friends of friends, or unsolicited connections. Attackers may attempt to friend you with introductions like "we met on vacation last year," "I was at that conference with you," "I'm a friend of your spouse/kid/family," or something like that. Unfortunately, social platforms are not always good at distinguishing between close, trusted friends, and distant, untrusted acquaintances.
- **Watch your postings.** When you post online, it is forever, and when you post personal information online it is forever compromised. Do not post personal identifying information like your home address, phone number, birthdate, place of birth, parent's names, social security numbers, or other data. When you post pictures online, or shoot a video in your home, look carefully to make sure personal information does not appear. Even a college diploma in

the background may be identifying, after it is frozen in the frame, zoomed in, and enhanced. Watch out for prescription drug bottles, as their labels may contain your address, phone number, medical conditions, insurance numbers, and other sensitive personal information.

- **Protect your games.** Online and mobile games are frequently free to play, but rapidly entice you to purchase premium content within the game. This enticement may be for additional tools, expansion modules, bonus levels, or "skins" for your online character. The game providers can make significant money from these premium offerings. At the same time the providers can collect (and store) your payment information, along with your online profile and friend network. Give careful attention to whom you are providing payment information, and do not let it fall into the wrong hands. Also, your online game purchases may result in license keys that are linked to your account online or sent to you via e-mail. These keys and corresponding online currencies can be worth hundreds of dollars and should be safeguarded accordingly.
- **Gaming "friends."** Gaming has become a social activity with entire leagues forming up around popular games. While many people play games with their real-world friends, people also make friends inside the virtual game worlds. These people may be in different states or different countries. Gaming connections may be powerful ones because of the shared gaming experience. However, these people are just as much strangers as anyone else one might meet online. Be wary, especially when kids or young adults are involved.
- **Gambling.** While online gambling is illegal in many countries (like the United States), that illegality has not stopped online gambling from becoming wildly successful. While many gambling sites are legitimate businesses, plenty more are not. Use caution and do research before giving up your credit card information online at these sites, and manage your gambling carefully within responsible limits.

Reducing Risk of Online Shopping, Credit Cards, Banking, and Automated Teller Machines

When we shop online, we invariably give up considerable personal information. Until digital cash truly becomes a commonly-used currency, the preferred way of purchasing online is with credit or debit cards. Home delivery of physical goods involves giving the merchant our address and accompanying telephone number. Put the personal information all together—address, phone number, credit or debit card, e-mail address, and maybe a password—and the merchant knows a lot about us and has almost everything necessary to steal our identity. In fact, professional identity thieves take this data and cross-reference it with data from other sites and breaches to make meta-profiles that can include hundreds of fields of data about you, your finances, and your accounts

To reduce the risk of your online shopping, credit cards, banking, and Automated Teller Machine (ATM) usage, you should consider the following:

- **Online shopping.** Choose carefully which websites you use for online shopping. When you shop at smaller or unusual websites, consider using third-party payment providers like PayPal, rather than giving the site your credit card directly. Be careful when you create an account at a site, and do not re-use passwords that are also used to access sensitive e-mail, online banking, or credit card accounts.
- **Watch out for fraudulent charges.** Do not use debit cards for online purchases, as the compromise of a debit card can endanger your entire bank account. You may also have less recourse with fraudulent debit card charges than you do with credit cards. Scrutinize your credit card and bank statements for possible fraud. You may also want to set up a separate credit card account, just for online purchases.
- **EMV payment and tap-and-pay.** Modern credit cards include microchip technology from the *Europay*, *Mastercard*, *Visa* consortium. This "EMV" technology uses a chip embedded in the credit or debit card to authorize transactions and verify your identity. The chip is almost impossible to duplicate, unlike the legacy magnetic stripe that preceded it. This EMV technology is slowly being required for credit card purchases worldwide, including the United States. Your personal information is much safer when you use EMV for your credit card purchases. If a personal identification number (PIN) is required to authorize the transaction, it is even more secure, but you should use caution to cover your hand when you key in your PIN. "Tap-and-pay" features are very convenient for quick purchases like for gasoline but are vulnerable to exploitation by attackers who can connect to your card's wireless features remotely. To protect against such fraud, your wallet or purse should be shielded to protect your card from snooping.
- **Snooping, skimmers, and ATMs.** Snooping involves watching your card transactions to read your card numbers and PIN codes. Skimming involves modifying terminals to steal a copy of your card's information, including the card number, your name, and other data. Skimmers may also capture your PIN entry. ATMs are particularly vulnerable to these types of attacks, because they are frequently out in the open and relatively unprotected. Skilled attackers have even succeeded in installing skimmers at major retailers, by pre-

tending to be maintenance personnel or installing their equipment after hours. Watch for obviously modified credit card terminals or ATMs, cameras watching the screen of ATMs you use (looking over your shoulder) and shield your hand when you enter your PIN codes.

Protecting Online Medical Privacy

Some of the most dangerous identity theft taking place has to do with medical information and medical payment information. Attackers who compromise your medical information may be able to make financial transactions in your name, buy medications in your name, and request thousands of dollars in insurance payments, all using your identity and medical coverage. Fraud in this area has exploded in the past decade, and increasing medical costs and complexity means the end of this fraud is nowhere in sight. Medical identity theft may also be dangerous, as medical records may become distorted by fraudulent transactions. Fraudulent transactions in your medical records may lead to incorrect diagnoses or conflicting medications, jeopardizing your health and safety. Finally, medical privacy is important, as inappropriate release of personal medial information may result in embarrassment or endanger your employment.

To reduce your risk of medical fraud, and to protect your online medical privacy, you should consider the following:
- **Understand the risks.** Medical fraud is real, and very expensive. This fraud is perpetuated by using stolen identities. Unfortunately, these risks are increased every time we allow our health insurance card to be copies by a service provider or fill out an extensive patient history form. Much of the risk is unavoidable, which is frustrating for everyone.
- **Protect your health care identity.** Safeguard your health care ID card just like a government ID or credit card. These cards are worth money to fraudsters! Look after them, do not loan them out, and report if they are lost or stolen. Shred your health care statements, both from health care providers and from your insurance, when they are no longer needed.
- **Check your health care statements and records.** When you are treated, you should get two statements—one from the service provider, and one from your insurance. The information on these statements should match, indicating the service you received matches what your insurance paid. *It is up to you to check this, as no one else knows what happened.* If you see a discrepancy, investigate and report it. The discrepancy could affect your payments, your deductibles, your treatment, and your safety. Also, check your medical records for accu-

racy. When records incorrectly indicate a condition you do not have, or a treatment you did not receive, it could be a sign of fraud or identity theft. It could also contribute to potentially life-threatening medical mistakes.

- **Report fraud when you see it.** If you find inappropriate charges from a health care provider, request an investigation. Escalate to government regulators if the response you get is inadequate. It may not be "your money," but the damage impacts all of us and the medical costs we all bear together.

Understanding Net Neutrality, HIPAA, and GDPR

Many of us would like to think the government "has our back" when we use the internet for pleasure or commerce. Unfortunately, we forget people were driving cars for more than *fifty years* before seatbelts were required by law in the United States. Yes, the government cares, but it moves at government speed, which is usually considerably slower than internet speed. Government regulations adopted today frequently address the security and privacy issues of last year, or a decade ago. Frankly, it is difficult for the legislators and regulators to keep up. We need to be aware that behavior that is *bad* online may not actually be *illegal*, unless it has been outlawed under more general crimes like "fraud," "theft," or "extortion."

In understanding the legality or illegality of online behaviors, we should consider the following:

- **Internet crime.** Most illegal online activities are illegal due to laws that have been on the books for years, or even decades. They fall under categories like financial theft, extortion, or mail fraud. Many computer "hacking" activities are outlawed under the Computer Fraud and Abuse Act (CFAA) passed back in 1984, and amended several times since then.
- **Net neutrality.** This area is a hot topic in the United States at the time of this writing, as legislation requiring ISPs to allow all network traffic to flow freely expired without a replacement in place. Without this requirement, ISPs can give preferential treatment to their content or that of their content partners. They could even completely block access to their competitors or websites they view as being "inappropriate." Many citizens consider this lack of net neutrality to be a dangerous limitation on personal freedom and privacy.
- **HIPAA.** The Health Insurance Portability and Accountability Act of 1996 (HIPAA) laid out many of the requirements for health care providers in terms of collecting medical information, sharing medical information, and protecting that information when it is stored on paper and online. Many of the hos-

pital and health care provider cyber protections can be directly traced back to this legislation and its requirements.

–   **GDPR.** The EU's General Data Protection Regulation (GDPR) is a comprehensive regulation requiring organizations to safeguard personal data and personal privacy for EU citizens. Because of the international nature of e-commerce, this legislation affects e-commerce worldwide, even outside of the EU. One of the more interesting aspects of this legislation is a requirement for a "forget me" feature that allows citizens to ask that their data be removed from an organization's records.

There are many more regulations worldwide regarding computer security, online commerce, and personal privacy. These regulations are changing almost daily as governments try to keep up with the rapid pace of change and newly emerging threats. Be aware of the situation in your country or state and understand your rights and responsibilities with regard to these laws and regulations.

Chapter 10
Protecting Yourself on Travel

Travel. The mere mention of the word tends to generate a range of emotional responses. For some, it conjures exciting images of strange foreign lands and exotic hotels. For others, it garners thoughts of logistical challenges, jetlagged exhaustion, and dreadful uncertainties. Few people are indifferent to travel, its many challenges, and its many opportunities. As shown in Figure 10.1, when traveling, you may use portable storage, mobile devices, or laptop computers to travel with your data and connect to your workplace or home. You are also likely connecting to the internet using Wi-Fi or cellular networks that are available on your trip and managed by someone else.

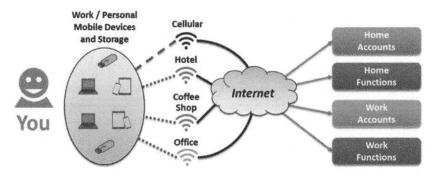

Figure 10.1: On travel, you are especially vulnerable because you are in unfamiliar locations using mobile information technology that is inherently less protected than at work or home.

Regardless of the emotions, there are some logistical realities when we travel, especially when we travel with our computers and mobile devices. When we are at home and possibly commuting to work, we do not have to take everything with us, all the time. When we travel, our personal effects, money, information, and devices are more vulnerable than at home, because we must carry them with us and we are in unfamiliar locations and unusual situations. Also, when we travel, we have less of a support network available to us, should something go wrong and we need to recover.

This chapter considers the cybersecurity risks related to traveling with information technology, and how you can reduce those risks through preparation and planning.

DOI 10.1515/9781501506505-010

Selecting What to Take When You Travel

Just as you do not normally carry your passport to run errands at home, when you travel you should look at what you bring with you, from an equipment perspective as well as from an information perspective. Only take what you need, based on what you plan on doing during the trip. If you only need a couple of files, do not take a multi-terabyte external hard drive containing thousands of files. Instead, put the files you need on a thumb drive and take the thumb drive with you (after encrypting it, if the files are sensitive). If you are only going to be accessing one of your accounts, do not take a password file that could give access to hundreds of accounts. If you do not need access to work files while on travel, you may want to take a personal laptop or mobile device instead.

Some ideas to consider when selecting what you need to take with you when traveling include the following:

- **Laptops, mobile devices, and removable media.** Only take devices you will need when you travel. For removable media, consider purchasing separate media for travel, rather than taking devices containing thousands of files you definitely will not need. Check with your company before taking company equipment on personal travel, especially if the travel is international.
- **Sanitize your devices.** If you are taking personal or work devices like computers, mobile phones, or removable media, look at what files are on those systems. Consider removing sensitive files not be needed for the trip, and then reinstalling them after the trip is complete.
- **"Disposable" devices.** Consider getting a prepaid mobile phone when you travel internationally, rather than taking or relying on your personal phone. A prepaid phone can reduce your risk and avoid roaming charges.
- **Get roaming service.** Inquire with your mobile carriers about roaming and international service. You may be able to get international roaming, texting, and data for a nominal charge, if you purchase it ahead of time.
- **Powered off and locked up when not in use.** Put screen locks on all your computers and mobile devices, so hotel staff can not power them up or look at them when you are not present. Use hotel safes to lock up equipment not in use, or keep it with you on your person.
- **Leverage the cloud.** Keep additional files you might need in the cloud, using Microsoft, Apple, or Google shared drives, or a service like Dropbox. The cloud can also be a useful place to put backup copies of the files you take with you, in case your primary devices are lost or damaged.

Considering Backups and Contingencies for Travel

When you travel, things go wrong. Bags get lost, equipment gets dropped, and files get corrupted. As Murphy's Law says, "what can go wrong will go wrong" whether we plan for it or not. So, it behooves us to plan accordingly. We want to have multiple backups of our most critical information and identity documents, in case the originals get lost. It can be very frightening to find yourself all alone in a foreign country after being robbed of your wallet, money, and identification.

When preparing backups and contingencies for travel, you should consider the following factors:

– **Protect your wallet and travel documents.** If you are traveling with a partner, make sure each of you has separate sets of identifying papers, trip itineraries, money, and credit cards. Back each other up, and then have more backups in your bags. If you are traveling alone, take two complete wallets where each has an ID, separate credit card, cash, and other important documents. If your passport is lost or stolen, even an expired driver's license can be helpful for proving who you are to embassy officials. Make sure you have redundant copies of travel documents and itineraries, and the extras are stored separately from the originals.

– **Know where to go for help.** Think through where you can go for help, should things go wrong. Have phone numbers for local consular offices, tourist assistance offices, your hotel, and travel agent. Make sure someone back home has this information as well, so they can help you in an emergency. Think through how you might get help, money, and support should things go very wrong. If you are traveling on business, get the contact information for your company's security and travel offices, as well as those for your supervisor and management.

– **Backup your data.** Backup your electronic files before you begin your trip. Do not take anything with you that can not be replaced from a backup, if necessary. Of particular concern are pictures on your mobile phone, if they are not automatically backed up when you take them. If there are critical files on your laptop computer, make sure you have a second copy of those files on removable media, and maybe even a third copy stored in the cloud.

– **Digital versus paper.** If you are traveling on business for a contract negotiation, you might want to have a paper copy of the contract somewhere in your bag. The paper copy can not get accidentally erased. Conversely, consider taking digital photographs of your passport, itinerary, and tickets, and keeping them on your smartphone. It's all about redundancy because you never know what might go wrong.

Using Kiosk Computers and Public Internet Connections

When traveling overseas, you may find yourself needing to use "kiosk" computers to print airline tickets or documents, or using public Wi-Fi network connections at your hotel or restaurants, perhaps to avoid cellular roaming. These are all legitimate uses—after all, who takes a printer with them on a trip—but such use also increases your risk and must be considered accordingly. Kiosk computers are notoriously insecure and should be assumed to be compromised when you use them.

When using kiosk computers and public internet connections while on travel, it is helpful to consider the following:

– **Assume kiosk machines are compromised.** Assume kiosk computers you are using are compromised, and reduce your use accordingly. If you are printing files or travel papers, consider forwarding those documents to a less-sensitive e-mail account rather than using your primary or company e-mail account from kiosk computers. Consider using a thumb drive for your files, rather than accessing sensitive e-mail or online accounts from a kiosk computer. Write protect your thumb drive (some have this feature) so the kiosk machine can not try to infect it with malware. If you have to enter sensitive credentials, try to change them soon afterward from a trusted device.

– **Assume public networks are dangerous.** When you connect to public networks, you do not know who or what is connected to that network or monitoring your network traffic. Other computers on the same network may be able to scan your computer for vulnerabilities and attempt to compromise it. In addition, the network may be able to monitor everywhere you go and everything you do. Depending on the configuration, this monitoring may include intercepting your connections to trusted websites and intercepting username and password credentials.

– **Engage your device defenses.** On your devices, ensure your personal firewall is enabled along with other defenses like antimalware software. When using your device, watch for signs of attack—like unsolicited messages, unexpected invitations, pop-ups, or attempts to install software. If you have access to a virtual private network (VPN) connection, immediately connect to the VPN so your outbound traffic is private and encrypted. The VPN tunnel protects your computer's network connection, and your web browsing, from prying eyes.

– **Do not automatically connect.** Turn off Wi-Fi options to "automatically connect" to known wireless networks. Attackers often stand up malicious networks that use common names like "public Wi-Fi," "hotspot," "coffee shop," "lobby," or "guest." Prefer wireless networks that are password-protected over unprotected "open" networks, when possible.

– **Use your cellular hotspot.** When you have a powerful "3G" or "4G" smartphone with good signal quality, the phone can act as an internet service provider (ISP) that you can use instead of public Wi-Fi for your laptop computer (data and roaming charges may apply). Cellular data connections tend to generally be more secure and more private than public Wi-Fi. For sensitive online activity, your hotspot may be a more secure alternative. Just make sure you configure it with a strong password.

Considering Physical Protection, Personal Safety, and Electricity

Your personal safety is much more vulnerable on travel than at home. Frequent transitions—from air to ground to hotel to taxi to train—and having to keep all of your personal belongings with you at all times is challenging. An additional challenge when traveling internationally has to do with electricity. Different countries have different electric power—generally either 110 volts or 220 volts, and a variety of plug standards and connectors. Being on a trip with a dying phone and not having a working charger just adds stress to a difficult situation, especially when you realize the dying phone has your itinerary, hotel address, and flight boarding passes on it, and there are no other copies available.

When keeping track of your personal belongings and using electricity in different countries while on travel, it is helpful to consider the following:

– **Check with the authorities.** When traveling internationally check with the government (in the United States, www.state.gov) for guidance and warnings specific to the country and region to which you are going. If traveling on business, your company security office may have guidance for you as well. Find out the addresses and telephone numbers of the embassy and consular offices in the country you are visiting.

– **Protect your valuables.** When staying in hotels, consider the following priority list for your valuables:

1. Lock your valuables in the hotel or room safe, protected by a combination or password selected by you.

2. If no safe is available, place valuables in drawers or suitcases where they are out of sight and not obviously present. Check on your valuables when you enter or leave the room to make sure everything is in order. Remember to check the safe and all drawers before you check out.

3. When not locked in a safe place, carry your valuables with you. Avoid keeping wallets in bags or back pockets where they may be visible and pickpocketed or easily taken.

4. For personal or business computers, use carry cases that do not look like they contain computers. "High-tech" computer cases may be particularly obvious and should be avoided for sensitive travel.

- **Hotel fire safety.** For each place where you stay, including hotels, hostels, or houses, walk the fire escape route and make sure it actually leads to the outside of the building. Know the primary and alternate fire escape routes from your room and other places you will be visiting.

- **Bring spare batteries and chargers.** While it may not be feasible to carry a spare laptop battery or power adapter, external "USB batteries" are popular and can double or triple the endurance of your smartphone or mobile device. In addition, bring at least one spare charger and charging cable—they are small, lightweight, inexpensive, and indispensable if a proprietary plug gets damaged or lost. With the right cable, you should be able charge your phone from your laptop in a pinch. In addition, devices with "USB C" connectors may be able to both send and receive power from other devices, including external batteries.

- **Do not forget power plug adapters.** Today, most consumer electronics have "multi-voltage" digital power adapters that can accept power from basically anywhere in the world. This capability is a far cry from twenty years ago, when international travel required getting separate transformers and power adapters. However, wall plugs are not quite so standardized. It is important to find out what the plug standards are for each area you will visit and make sure you bring the appropriate adapters with you on the trip for all your electrical needs. You will end up needing them and trying to find them in the middle of a trip might be a challenge. If you forget, check with the hotel front desk—they may be able to help you out in a pinch.

Being Cautious about Conversations and Online Sensitive Data

When traveling, you do not know who is standing next to you or looking over your shoulder. This situation may be at the airport, on the plane, or in the lobby of your hotel. If you are traveling for work, the people sitting next to you at breakfast could work for the government, the customer, or the competition. In some countries, the government may be working directly with business, or may be monitoring your presence for myriad possible reasons. You just do not know. So, you want to be cautious about what you say, what you type, and what is visible on your device screens.

Screen locks, privacy screens, and awareness of shoulder surfing can help to reduce your risk on travel, considering the following factors.

– **Step outside or go back to the room.** You do not need to discuss your company's negotiating strategy in the lobby of the hotel, if you can avoid it. The same goes for reviewing account numbers with a family member back home who is trying to pay your credit card bill. If you need to have a private conversation regarding sensitive information, try to get away from potentially spying people, or go back to your room. If it appears that someone is following you as you move, end the conversation and make arrangements to continue the conversation later.
– **Lock your screen.** Install a screen lock on your laptop and mobile devices. Make sure the screen is locked if you have to step away, even if it is just for a minute. Configure the screen to automatically lock after a period of inactivity—say 15 minutes or so.
– **Install a privacy screen.** Privacy screens are available for laptop computers, as well as for mobile devices. Some privacy screens are removable, which can be helpful if you need to share a laptop screen sometimes, while staying private at other times. Privacy screens on a mobile device can make it much harder for prying eyes to see your accounts, contacts, logons, or phone numbers.
– **Beware of shoulder surfing.** When you are entering phone numbers, e-mail addresses, usernames, or passwords, be aware of the people around you. Who is sitting or standing behind you? Can they see your screen? Can they see your hands? Orient yourself so people are not behind you, and so your hands can not be easily seen while you are typing in sensitive information or accessing your online accounts.

Protecting Your Hard Drive and Mobile Media with Encryption

Any time you take large amounts of sensitive personal data outside your home or workplace, it should be protected. Maintaining physical control of all your devices at all times is difficult, if not impossible, when traveling. So, you should assume that other people can get access to your devices. We compensate for this by putting passwords on devices, but what about our storage? Even with a password-protected device, it may be possible to access the device's storage and copy its files. Removable hard drives and "thumb drives" are particularly easy to copy, perhaps in as little as a few minutes of unauthorized access. We can defend against these types of attacks by using encryption.

To use encryption to protect your mobile devices, laptop drives, and removable media, you should consider the following:

- **Mobile devices and remote wipe.** On your mobile devices, enable storage encryption for built-in and removable storage. This enablement is usually done by specifying a device "passcode" for access to the device. On Android, these features are usually in the "Security Settings" area and include options for encrypting the phone and microSD removable storage. On Apple's iOS, encryption is enabled by default once a passcode is put in place. You should also consider enabling "find my phone" and "remote wipe" functions available for your operating system.
- **Laptop drive encryption.** Whether your laptop has a conventional spinning hard drive or a solid-state drive (SSD) with no moving parts, drive encryption protects against someone removing the drive and simply copying its data. This type of attack is daunting because it does not matter what the operating system is, or what your password is to logon to the computer. By enabling drive encryption, the drive is not accessible until the user has entered the drive encryption password, prior to the computer starting up. In Windows, this enablement can be done using the built-in "BitLocker" drive encryption; Apple's version is called "FileVault;" and most Linux distributions include the "dm-crypt" and "LUKS" open source encryption tools.
- **Removable media encryption.** Removable hard drives and solid-state drives can be encrypted using the same tools as laptop computers. However, there may be additional challenges if the removable media is to be used with multiple computers or operating systems. If you encrypt your removable media, make sure all computers that may need to use that media have the appropriate software installed, or that you bring the software with you. Third-party tools from McAfee and Symantec include disk encryption tools that can work across multiple computer platforms, with a simple installation.
- **Backup, backup, backup.** The downside of drive encryption is that it may make data recovery from a failed drive difficult or even impossible, even if you have the password for the encryption. It also means a minor drive failure may make your computer unable to boot, even in "safe mode." It also means that data can be lost if the encryption key is deleted or forgotten. So, backups become more important when encryption is used. Make sure you have backups of your operating system, applications, and data.

Reducing the Risk of USB Connections

Universal serial bus (USB) was originally designed to allow a number of different interfaces between devices to be replaced by a single, universal connector plug and communication protocol. These interfaces included early serial, parallel, mouse, keyboard, multimedia, and external drive connectors. USB 1.0 was released in 1995 and dramatically reduced the number of ports that need to be supported by devices or operating systems. Instead of requiring multiple external interfaces and adapter cards, which was the norm before USB, a personal computer could simply have a couple of USB ports or USB "hubs" that allow even more peripherals to be attached to the ports that were available.

To support all of this flexibility, USB also included the ability to transmit power. This power output ranged from 0.5 watts in older devices all the way up to 100 watts using the latest protocol and special cables. The challenge of these capabilities is that by mixing power delivery with data delivery, it becomes possible for power plugs to talk to devices, and vice versa. The other challenge that has emerged, from a security perspective, is that USB devices can cause computers to dynamically install software drivers, possibly from untrusted sources. This means that untrusted USB devices may be able to install software into your operating system. As a consequence, you can never be 100% sure that a USB peripheral is talking to your computer or mobile device in a completely "appropriate" way. Security researchers have found instances where cyberattackers built USB devices that appeared to be thumb drives or power adapters, but were actually malicious peripherals that installed malware onto unsuspecting victim computers.

To reduce the risk of inappropriate or malicious USB connections and media while on travel, you should consider the following:
- **Bring your own USB chargers.** Bring your own USB devices, peripherals, and chargers. If you can avoid it, do not use USB ports at hotels or public places to charge your devices. It is just too easy to rewire these devices so they both charge *and* infect their customers. Use your own charger and plug it into an electrical wall socket.
- **Get thumb drives with write protect.** For file sharing, get thumb drives that include a "write protect" feature so that no malware can be written onto the drives when you plug them into an untrusted computer. Use the write protect feature when all you need to do is read the files contained on the drives. With a new thumb drive, reformat it completely before using it, and again after you have exposed it to untrusted computers or devices.
- **Beware of "free" USB devices.** While it may be convenient to get vendor information on a free thumb drive with the vendor's logo on it, these devices

can be easily infected in a number of ways (even from the factory). Unfortunately, cheap thumb drive manufacturing is incredibly competitive and quality control may be lacking. Also, there are many ways that malicious cyber attackers can use such "free" thumb drives to attempt to get past your computer's defenses, as discussed above.

Considering Diplomacy, ITAR, EAR, and Security Clearances

When you travel internationally you become a part of international diplomacy, whether you intend to or not. If you perform a crime or get arrested while overseas, your crime may turn into an international incident, where you become a pawn in geopolitical maneuvering. Similarly, you may run afoul of government laws and regulations, especially if you work for a government contractor, do government business, or have a security clearance issued by your government. In the United States, some of the regulations governing international travel include the International Traffic in Arms Regulations (ITAR) and Export Administration Regulations (EAR). In short, when you take data outside of your home country, you are exporting that data, even if you do not intend for it to stay overseas.

When thinking about diplomacy, ITAR, EAR, and security clearances with regard to international travel, you should consider the following:
- **Be aware of international laws and politics.** Different countries have different rules regarding data handling, merchandise for demonstration or samples, prescription drugs, and controlled substances. If you are traveling with prescription drugs—particularly narcotics—make sure you have all of the appropriate paperwork and doctor's orders with you. Understand what is allowed and not allowed crossing the border and in the country you are visiting. If you are confronted by the authorities, do not get belligerent, but also try to get help from your country's local consulate. Treat everyone respectfully and try to get others involved who are on your side.
- **Know if you handle export-controlled data.** If you are in a business that handles export-controlled data, or highly proprietary commercial data, know if you have it on your computer, removable media, or mobile device. Encryption does not protect data from export, and just taking a device with export-controlled data on it outside of the country may constitute export, even if you do not intend to leave it there. If in doubt, get another "clean" device that has never contacted export-controlled data. If you suspect someone tampered with your device while on travel, wipe your device clean and reinstall your operating system when you return.

- **Consult with your employer or security officer.** If you have a security clearance, you may be required to report international travel beforehand, and then submit a post-trip report afterward. If you handle export-controlled or highly sensitive data, your company may want you to report international travel, regardless. Contact your security office and follow their guidance.
- **Watch out for other confidential and proprietary data.** You should consider what other confidential and/or proprietary data you have, and if you should take that data with you. If you are visiting a company, do you have data from that company's competitor as well? It would be terribly embarrassing if that data were to leak, even by accident. Such embarrassment could be career-limiting for you, if it turns out you could have prevented it.
- **Be cautious and have contingency plans.** As is often the case with travel, it pays to be cautious and plan for things that could go wrong. Make sure people know you are traveling, and can contact the authorities if you go missing or something happens to you. What if you have an accident—will someone be able to find you at the hospital? Accidents are scary enough when they are at home, where we have family and friends available to help us. Do not take unnecessary risks, do not be a daredevil, and be prepared for things that could go wrong. Above all else, be considerate of your surroundings, as you are a guest to their country and an ambassador for your own country.

Chapter 11
When Things Go Wrong

Despite our best efforts and intentions, things go wrong. Phones get dropped in water, laptops fall off tables, hard drives and power supplies fail. Cyberthreats do not change the fact that it is a dangerous world out there; they just add another dimension of danger to existing, day-to-day threats. So, we need to assume things will go wrong, and plan accordingly. An additional wrinkle cyberthreats introduce into this planning is that we may find ourselves up against a deliberate attacker who is trying to do us wrong. An attacker who will try to defeat the measures we put in place for protection, detection, and recovery. To compensate, we need to be extra careful and plan accordingly.

Planning includes assessing risks you may encounter, thinking through how you will manage those risks, and identifying the possibilities of what can go wrong. In general terms, some of the major possible incidents include the following:
–   **Your devices' data is breached.** Private data on your personal devices is stolen by an attacker, who then attempts to use that data against you.
–   **Your devices are damaged or destroyed.** The software, storage, or hardware of your devices is damaged. As a result, your applications, accounts and/or data are not available to you.
–   **Your online accounts are compromised.** Your online accounts are compromised, giving attackers access to those accounts, including the ability to change passwords and hijack those accounts from you.
–   **Your data is changed.** Your personal data is altered, or false data is posted in your name. This could result in fraudulent transactions, scandalous postings, or inappropriate online or social media connections made in your name.
–   **Something happens to you or your significant others.** Something happens to you, and those who are dependent on you can not access your accounts. Or something happens to your significant others and you can not access accounts in their names.

This chapter describes some of the ways that things can go wrong from a cybersecurity perspective and provides suggested actions you can take to reduce your risk and improve your recovery.

DOI 10.1515/9781501506505-011

Being Prepared

As the old Scouting motto says, "Be Prepared." It behooves everyone to think through the possibilities for harm and think of ways to prepare for those possibilities. While an ounce of prevention may beat a pound of cure, when prevention fails it is smart to have a pound of cure on hand, just in case. If something goes wrong, you or someone else may have to reconstruct your digital life. That includes your devices, your accounts, your applications, and your data. Being prepared includes being able to reconstruct all of them in the event something goes horribly wrong.

To be prepared for when things go wrong, you should consider taking the following actions:
- **Inventory your devices.** Inventory your IT devices which may include: desktop and laptop computers, tablets, mobile phones, cameras, portable drives, memory chips, and thumb drives.
- **Inventory your accounts and passwords.** Make a list of your online accounts and passwords. If you use a password manager, make sure it is in the inventory. Make sure your loved ones know where this list is and update it when your accounts change.
- **Know where your data resides.** Where are the originals of your most important data? Where are the copies? Which data is automatically copied to the cloud? Do your old phones and tablets have irreplaceable data on them, because you never backed them up?
- **Consolidate your data.** When you have photographs in ten different locations, it is hard to protect them. Consolidate your most important and most irreplaceable data into one or two places so it is easy to manage, and then arrange to back it up regularly and robustly.
- **Back up your data regularly.** Back up your important data and files. For your most important files, make a backup copy periodically—say once a quarter—and store the backup offline in a safety deposit box or something similar. Update those backups regularly so they stay current, but be careful of incremental backups that can introduce complex dependencies between backup files. Encrypt your backups but make sure you have or know the keys for data recovery.
- **Back up your data again.** If your data is really important, back it up multiple times. Some experts recommend that the most important data be backed up at least *three* times: (1) the original file, (2) an online backup that may be automatically performed, and (3) an offline archive that is isolated and

protected. This approach guards against a single incident taking out both the original and the backup, all at once.

- **Understand the limits of automatic backup.** Automatic and cloud-based backup are useful for automatically making extra copies of your files separate from the originals. "File history" backups can even keep track of different versions of your files, so you can undo changes to a favorite photo or lookup older versions of a document. However, these technologies provide limited protection against an attacker who is intent on destroying your data. Advanced malware and ransomware will attempt to damage the online backups as well as the originals.

- **Back up your devices and applications.** Make sure you have backups that allow you to "restore" your computers, their operating systems, and applications to their original configurations (also known as, "bare metal" backups). Update these backups if your hardware changes, or when you install new software. You may want to keep more than one bare metal backup on hand in case one of them becomes corrupted.

- **Organize your backups.** Another challenge is organization for backups. A good technique is to name backups based on: (1) the date the backup was made; (2) the name of the device backed up; and (3) the type of the backup. Backup types may include "bare metal," "application data," "personal files," or something similarly descriptive.

- **Test your backups.** Countless enterprises and many more individuals have found out too late the backup they thought they had was useless. Occasionally connect your backup devices and make sure they work, and you can read them. You probably do not want to test a "bare metal" restore on your computer, but you should at least check that the data is there. Backup drives that are more than five years old should probably be replaced with newer media, even if the older drives still work.

- **Have contingency plans.** Have options in case the primary contingency backup plan does not work, and maybe even backup options after that. This includes having more than one backup of your data. Have paper copies of password sheets, in case the digital versions are unavailable. Have your software installation discs and license keys, in case a "bare metal" restore fails.

Recognizing Dangerous Attacks

Unfortunately, it is seldom obvious when your devices or accounts are hacked. Just as your car seldom tells you exactly what is wrong with it, you will likely have to do some analysis of the symptoms to determine if something has gone wrong with your computer or device, and if those problems have to do with hacking or compromise. Symptoms may vary widely and diagnosing a symptom may be challenging or inconclusive. Do your best and seek out more experienced expertise if you are in doubt.

To recognize dangerous attacks against your computers and devices, you should consider the following possible symptoms:

- **Malicious pop-ups.** When browsing the web, you may run into pop-up windows designed to deceive you, either by telling you to update your computer's software or telling you your computer has been hacked. These are *not* signs of compromise! These are signs you have stumbled into a malicious website or malvertising. Only be concerned if the windows continue appearing after you have closed your browser and restarted your computer.
- **Ransomware screens.** Ransomware is one of the few malicious attacks that announces its arrival. If your computer is infected with ransomware, it will announce to you quite clearly that your system is being held ransom, and the steps you need to take to decrypt it. Whether or not you pay the ransom is a personal decision. Just be aware you may not get your data back, even if you do pay up.
- **Ransomware encryption.** While it is encrypting your system, ransomware replaces regular files with encrypted versions of those files. This process can take several hours, so it is possible you will be sitting in front of your computer while it is being encrypted. You may notice that some of your files have become encrypted and the hard drive or solid-state drive (SDD) are showing heavy, nonstop activity. If you see this activity, one technique is to turn off your computer at the power switch to stop the encryption process. By aborting the encryption process, you may be able to retrieve your other files that had not yet been encrypted. Note that this does not work for all ransomware strains, and may require considerable technical expertise to recover the remaining unencrypted files.
- **Strange startup programs and browser plug-ins.** When you first start up your computer, there should be very little running except for the operating system. Check your operating system's "startup programs" list and make sure you recognize all of them, or they make sense. For example, Windows 10 allows you to manage your startup programs, by going to Settings > Apps > Startup. You will see a list of "Startup Apps" designated to run automatically when you sign into your computer. You can configure which apps you want to automatically start. The same goes for web browser plug-ins. Check your web browser's documentation for how to configure which plug-ins are installed and enabled.

- **Changed web browser home page.** Malvertisers and click fraud attacks may change your browser home page. By changing your browser home page to their customers' pages, malvertisers generate page views and clicks that translate directly into fraudulent advertising revenue for them and their partners.
- **Malware alerts.** If your antimalware software alerts you of malicious software, take it seriously. If you suspect malware, open your antimalware program directly from your operating system and follow its instructions from there. Do not rely on a pop-up window, as the pop-up may be malicious and designed to deceive you.
- **Unusual program installs.** Periodically, check the programs installed on your computer or device. Do you remember installing that software? Do you know what that software does? Can you find the program in your "Start" or "Applications" menu to be able to run it? If in doubt, do some research on the program to see if you can understand what it does. Remove applications you do not recognize, or no longer need.
- **High central processing unit, disk, or battery usage.** Heavy usage of your central processing unit (CPU), disk, or battery may be a sign of malware. For example, "cryptoware" malware surreptitiously uses your computer to mine cryptocurrency, potentially resulting in high resource usage. Ransomware uses large amounts of resources while it is encrypting your files. Botnet malware may use resources to launch distributed denial of service (DDoS) attacks from your device. Other viruses and worms may use resources scanning your network or replicating themselves across it. On mobile devices, this activity may rapidly drain your battery—examining your battery usage may reveal the offending malicious app.
- **This list is just a start.** Unfortunately, this list of dangers is just a start, and plenty of malware can elude basic detection by hiding in the registry, in boot records, in hardware non-volatile memory, and other places. Other sophisticated malware may "throttle" its resource usage so it is hard to recognize that malicious software is running. Stealthy malware can be almost impossible to find, and attackers are coming up with new concealment techniques all the time.

Recognizing Account Compromise

Perhaps even worse than compromise of our devices is compromise of our online accounts. Every year, seemingly more and more of our digital life is contained in our online accounts, whether it is online pictures, connections with friends, or business and financial accounts. When these accounts are compromised, all of that capability is placed in jeopardy, and someone else has control of some aspect of our digital life. Sometimes, these attacks may result in fraudulent transactions or criminal behavior. Other times, they just mean we have to change our passwords or online credentials to reduce the risk of further compromise or possible damages down the road.

To recognize when your online accounts are compromised, it is helpful to consider the following factors:
- **E-mail notifications.** Sometimes, we find out our accounts have been compromised through a notification from the account operator. Unfortunately, these types of notifications are popular with fraudsters, so they may be malicious, too. If you receive an e-mail notification that one of your online accounts has been compromised, go directly to the account's website (*do not click on the link*) and login. If the notification was legitimate and the site is using good practices, you will be prompted to change your password when you logon. Go ahead and change your password. If it is a password you use elsewhere, you should change it everywhere you use it.
- **Compromise in the press.** Sometimes the press may cover a breach that does not directly affect you or where you are not notified by the account operator. Similarly, you may see a site such as www.havibeenpwned.com showing that your account has been compromised. When a breach occurs, use your judgment – it is always safer to change your credentials when it is possible they have been compromised, than to leave them alone and be vulnerable.
- **Strange e-mails.** If your friends report receiving strange e-mails from you or you find strange e-mails in your sent or deleted items folders, it is a sign that your e-mail account has been hacked or compromised. The same goes if you receive strange e-mails from your friends. In all of these cases, consider changing the credentials on your e-mail account, and watch it carefully for further suspicious activity.
- **Account access or fraudulent transactions.** Many online services allow you to see a log of account logins or tell you when you last successfully logged in. You should review the logins to look for fraudulent transactions or activities. If you think you are a victim of fraudulent activities, consider changing your credentials, as well as any other uses of the same passwords elsewhere.

Responding to Online Personal Attacks

More disturbing than simple attacks against our computers or compromise of our accounts are personal attacks. These attacks are crimes committed against us as individuals. The attackers may know who we are, where we shop, or how we pay for purchases. They may have obtained access to our computers, data, or accounts. These attacks are almost always crimes of some sort, although they are seldom prosecuted due to the difficulty of tracking down online attackers.

When considering online personal attacks, you should think about the following factors:

- **Account hijacking, hostage, and ransom.** More malicious than simple account access is account hijacking. With hijacking, attackers deliberately take control of your accounts and try to deny you access to those same accounts. They may do this hijacking by changing the password and password reset parameters to values only they know. They may also take control of your e-mail accounts so they can control e-mail-based password reset mechanisms and notifications. When your accounts are hijacked, attackers may start racking up fraudulent charges or they may contact you with ransom demands. In all of these cases, you will likely need to contact your accounts' customer service to prove your identity and get assistance. You may also need to involve law enforcement, depending on the amount of monetary damage. Do not expect getting the situation resolved to be easy or quick.
- **Blackmail and extortion.** Similar to account hijacking, criminals may attempt to blackmail you or extort you through compromise of your computers, devices, or accounts. In these cases, they will most likely contact you with their demands. Usually this blackmail is via e-mail but it may be through social media. While their demands will frequently be monetary, it is not always the case. Sometimes, you may be simply a stepping stone toward "bigger fish" in your social network or at your employer. In all of these cases, you should get help from professionals, law enforcement, and your accounts' customer service departments. You should also include your company security office, if you suspect the incident is employment-related.
- **Cyberbullying and revenge porn.** Online intimidation takes many forms. Cyberbullying involves bullying and intimidating the victim online in chat rooms, on social media, or by defacing personal postings with slanderous comments or counter-postings. Revenge porn involves obtaining access to personal pictures or videos from webcams or mobile devices, and then posting those images or videos online. Frequently, these actions are performed by someone known and trusted by the victim—or at least previously

trusted. These actions can be frightening and intimidating and are frequently criminal. You can reduce your vulnerability to these types of attacks by being careful where you post and what you say. Regarding revenge porn, do not keep highly personal photos on your computers, connected devices, or online accounts. Cover up your webcam when it is not in use. If you think you are a victim, contact law enforcement.

Locking Down Online Accounts

If your computers, devices, or online accounts are infected or compromised, you should immediately try to "lock down" your online accounts, so they can not be used by attackers. Malware frequently tries to steal credentials for popular online services, including e-mail, social media, banking, e-commerce, and gaming. Some malware can recognize when you go to one of these websites and will then monitor your keyboard to detect when you have entered in your online credentials and passwords. The malware then sends your online credentials and passwords out to its controllers, who aggregate this type of data for millions of victims and then sell it to other criminal groups to exploit. It is big business. So, if you suspect you have been compromised, one of the first things you should do is regain control of your online accounts. You may want to try to do this even before you try to clean up the malware on your computer. That is, provided you have another computer or device you can use to do the locking down.

When you need to lock down your online accounts, you should consider the following factors:

- **Use a trusted device.** The first rule of locking down your accounts is you need to do it from a device that is trusted. If your main computer has been compromised, maybe you can lock down your accounts from your smartphone, or another computer. Be cautious using another computer in the same household, as malware may "jump" to other computers on the same network. Malware frequently has difficulty replicating between different types of devices—like from a Windows PC to an Apple Mac, or from Android to iOS—so if the devices are different operating systems your risk is lower. Make sure you can access the accounts in question from your device, and that you have all necessary apps, bookmarks, or multifactor authentication tools in place to logon to your accounts and configure them. Another option may be to contact your provider's customer service and ask for assistance.
- **Do it as soon as possible.** Once you have identified a trusted device to work from, start changing passwords as quickly as possible. Start with your pass-

word manager (if you have one) and your e-mail accounts, as they tend to be key to doing password resets and "lost password" functions for your other accounts. Then, consider accounts in terms of their monetary or personal value and change credentials for the most important ones first. For all password resets, use care to go directly to the website for the account or service, and use the password reset function there. Do not go to it from e-mail messages or other links.

- **Check your password reset settings and identity questions.** As you log in to accounts and change your passwords, check the settings for the accounts, especially registered e-mail addresses, telephone numbers, and identity verification questions. Make careful note of any data you will not immediately recall—including passwords if necessary. If you use a password manager, make sure you update passwords there as well. If you have multiple e-mail accounts, make sure you know which e-mail addresses are tied to which of your accounts. Keep notes if necessary.

- **Watch out for password reset e-mail messages.** As you change your passwords, you should receive e-mail messages from your accounts indicating you had changed your credentials. Make sure you get these e-mail messages, and they look correct. If you change an account and do not get a password reset e-mail message, double-check the e-mail account associated with your account is correct. It is possible, but unlikely, your account holders do not send password reset notifications.

- **Consider turning on fraud alerts and multifactor.** Some accounts may permit you to activate multifactor authentication using cell phone messaging, Duo Security software, or other additional factors. Financial accounts may also permit you to put a "fraud alert" or other safeguard onto your account. Consider the possible benefits and challenges of using multifactor authentication or fraud protections, if only temporarily.

- **Do not get locked out.** It is easy to end up locking yourself out of your own accounts, if you are not careful. It is even easier if an attacker is actively wrestling with you for ultimate control of your online accounts. Be careful, and make sure you have control of your password managers and e-mail accounts first. These accounts will serve as the identity foundation you use to control access to your other accounts. If they are re-compromised, you may have to start all over again to reset everything.

- **Be prepared to lock down accounts multiple times.** Do not assume you are going to get it right the first time and use your "second-most-favorite-clever-password" everywhere. Unfortunately, the days of having one single "super key" to your online identity are rapidly coming to an end. You will likely run into issues with timing, password policies, and password reuse requirements that make your password selections considerably more complex. Make careful notes for your accounts and do not hesitate to re-change passwords for accounts that are problematic or appear to be at further risk of compromise.

- **Make note of customer service numbers.** For many of your online accounts, there are customer service lines where you can get a real live person to help you, at least during business hours. Know what these phone numbers are and be prepared to prove your identity to their customer service representatives or to argue that your identity has been hijacked. Financial institutions may even set up separate identity verification criteria for over the phone, which may be useful if your online accounts are compromised or need to be locked down. Alternatively, you may be able to submit a customer support request online, and someone will call you back.

Resetting Your Compromised Computer or Device

Malware on a computer or device is a scary situation. Once a computer or device has been compromised, every file contained on it, and every keystroke into it becomes suspect. Is my computer recording me? Is it broadcasting everything I do? Is it trying to compromise the rest of my network, or my social circle? These are questions that should be considered once the original compromise has occurred. While cybersecurity capabilities have improved over the past decade, there still is not a universal "clean up" button on computers or mobile devices to restore them immediately back to a known good configuration. Some level of finesse is required to balance a number of tradeoffs to get your computer or device back to a relatively safe configuration, while reducing the amount of pain and time involved in the process.

If you suspect your computer or device has been compromised, you should consider the following factors:

- **Unplug from the network.** By disconnecting from the network, you make it impossible for malware to communicate with "command and control" servers that may be instructing it on what to do. While disconnecting the network connection does not defeat the malware, it stops the malware from reporting your activities and getting new instructions. Once you are unplugged, you should still be able to perform most of the procedures described in this section while remaining disconnected.
- **Use your antimalware "clean" function.** Some malicious software is caught by antimalware software and can then be quarantined and "cleaned up." Some antimalware like Windows Defender also has an "offline" function

that may be able to remove malware embedded within the operating system. Note that while these features are useful, they may not always be effective; some malware is specifically designed to defeat them.

- **Address ransomware.** If your computer has been infected with ransomware, special procedures can apply. If you could stop the ransomware before its installation is completed, and your antimalware software detected the malware, you may be able to clean up your system and restore damaged files from backups. Even if you were not successful in stopping the encryption, the "No more ransom" project may have some help for you at their website https://www.nomoreransom.org. The worst-case scenario is you may have to reinstall your system and your data from a backup. Watch out for ransomware that encrypts your cloud backups, and attempts to reinfect you from there as well. Microsoft's OneDrive and other cloud services include anti-ransomware features that may help to protect you and your data from these attacks.
- **Uninstall the program or app.** If you can identify the malware as being related to a specific program or app you installed (or that was installed for you), go ahead and remove the program or app. While this approach is hardly guaranteed, it can defeat many forms of "adware," "spyware," and some free programs that are somewhat malicious but not particularly dangerous.
- **Disable startup programs or browser plug-ins.** Similarly, you may be able to trace the behavior to a specific startup program or browser plug-in. If this is the case, go ahead and disable it, reboot your computer, and see if it stays removed. If your symptoms disappear, then you may be okay. If the malware comes back, then you may have a larger problem requiring security support personnel to get involved.
- **Modify the registry.** Some malware hides in the operating system "registry" that contains system configuration settings, or in other files used when the computer starts up. While it is possible to remove such malware, these actions are nontrivial and may render your system unusable. Use care if you choose to do something like this approach yourself.
- **Computer system restore point.** Your operating system may have a "system restore point" function that allows you to "roll back" the operating system to a known-good configuration. This feature removes programs and operating system changes made since the selected restore point, but generally leaves your files and settings intact. If you know approximately when your problems started, you can use this feature to reconfigure your system. You will likely have to manually reinstall any legitimate programs that were installed since the restore point. Be careful not to reinstall the malware!
- **Computer "bare metal" restore.** If a system restore does not work, but you still have an idea of when your system was last "good," you may be able to

do a "bare metal" restore from a backup that was made before the problem occurred. This approach, of course, assumes that you are making regular backups of your operating system and programs. Note that a bare metal restore will likely *not* preserve your personal files, so they may have to be recovered separately. Recovering your personal files separately may make a bare metal restore more disruptive than a computer operating system reset, described below.

– **Computer operating system reset.** Operating systems like Windows 10 and MacOS have a "reset your operating system" feature. This feature completely reinstalls your operating system, while leaving your personal files intact. The downside of this approach is that while your files are retained, it removes *all* of your applications. So, you will have to reinstall your applications from the original media or downloads. However, preserving your personal files may be more important. Make sure you have your license keys!

– **Mobile device factory reset.** Many mobile devices have a "factory reset" function that resets the operating system back to its "factory" configuration when you got the device new. This feature only takes a couple of minutes to reset the operating system, but will also delete all your files and apps. While apps can usually be reinstalled from the app store relatively easily, your personal data must be backed up to the cloud or to another device. Incidentally, this reset function is useful for giving your used mobile device to charity, or to another family member.

– **Computer system rebuild.** If an operating system reset does not work, you may have to do a complete system rebuild. If this is the case, you may also need to check your system's motherboard firmware, as some attacks can even modify the firmware to survive even a complete system rebuild. Rebuilding your system involves reformatting your system's hard drive or solid-state drive (SSD) and then reinstalling the operating system and applications from scratch. Personal files can then be restored from backups or secondary copies. This approach is a major undertaking and generally should be a last resort.

– **Computer firmware reset.** Some malware can even infect the BIOS firmware in the motherboard and some peripherals. Such sophisticated malware may require extensive cleanup including reflashing of firmware memory, replacement of peripherals, or replacement of the computer hardware altogether. These undertakings are complex, risky, and non-trivial—nontechnical users should collaborate with experienced security professionals or support staff.

– **Backups and spare drives.** In many of these scenarios, before you make a bad situation worse by removing programs, changing registry keys, or wiping hard drives, you may want to make additional backups to protect yourself should things get worse. "Clone" your system hard drive so you can work on a copy of the original, while still being able to go back to the original should the recovery attempt fail. This situation is where having multiple backups is wise; it is easy to completely destroy the system you are trying to recover. It is far better to have a compromised copy of your files that is intact than it is to have destroyed all your copies in a recovery attempt gone awry. Use extreme caution, take your time, have extra copies, and do not hesitate to ask for help.

Recovering Lost Data

Once you have restored your computer or device, the next step is to restore your data to that device. Your data takes many forms, including configuration settings, preferences, favorites, bookmarks, accounts, passwords, and of course files. Files can include documents you have downloaded, documents and messages you created, pictures you created, photos you captured, and media files like music or movies. If you must completely rebuild your computer or replace your device, you may have to recover or replace all of these types of documents to get back to where you were before whatever incident occurred. Each category of data has different patterns of creation, maintenance, use, and change. These different patterns are factors in identifying the best ways to save and recover your data, should you need to do so.

When planning to recover your data as part of rebuilding your system or device, you should consider the following factors:

– **Where the data comes from.** Where did the data originally come from? Was the data e-mailed to you or did you download it from the internet? Does the data consist of documents you created yourself, or edited? The documents you created or the pictures you took are often considered some of the most valuable data you have. Those documents and pictures may be irreplaceable if you do not have them backed up. Make sure you back up the data you create when you create it, or soon thereafter.
– **How often the data changes.** For documents you actively modify, including e-mail archives, software development, photos you take, or personal documents, you should think about how often they change. If you are making daily changes to files, you need to make sure you are backing them up daily, as well.
– **When and where the data has been backed up.** Where are your backups? Which backups are online or offline? When was the most recent backup made? Did you e-mail files or post them to the internet? Frequently, your most

recent copies of files may be in e-mail or online in document shares or posted to social media. Do not underestimate the power of e-mailing something to yourself as a backup mechanism, or asking friends for copies of materials you had sent them previously.

- **The integrity of the backups.** Which backups are intact and which are corrupted? Frequently, ransomware attempts to encrypt backups that are online, so you may find your most recent backups to be unusable. If this situation occurs, you need to look into alternative offline backups, as well as contingency locations for your favorite files. Make sure you understand what backups are usable or not, and have contingencies for important files that were changed recently but you still want to be able to recover.

- **Ease and convenience of recovery.** You will likely find yourself facing some difficult tradeoffs when doing a large-scale data recovery. Do you get that hard drive out of your safe deposit box from last year, or do you ask your cousin to send you that "in case of emergency" thumb drive from six months ago? Or are the 15 gigabytes in your cloud drive "good enough" for now? Consider the tradeoffs and make the choices that are best for you.

- **Single points of failure.** After a failure occurs, you are in a vulnerable state since you have lost one or more of your stores for important personal data and documents. Be careful your recovery effort does not leave you with "single points of failure" that could cause you to lose a decade of documents should a second failure occur. It may be prudent to make additional copies of your backups immediately, just to give you redundancy. In other words, make sure you restore your redundancy as soon as possible, to guard against future mishaps.

- **Data comparison tools.** In a recovery situation, you will likely find yourself in a situation of having multiple copies of documents, messages, pictures, videos, or other documents. You will probably have folders containing hundreds or even thousands of documents. You may need to determine which of them contains the most documents, the most recent documents, or the most useful documents. Comparison tools like "windiff" and "kaleidoscope" can help you to compare large numbers of files quickly to find differences and determine which documents to keep. Other tools can help you find duplicate copies of documents and photos, so you do not have to keep multiple copies of the same file. Use these tools to organize your data and reduce duplication.

Reporting Work Cyber Incidents

If you access your work accounts from a personal device—which many of us do—compromise of your personal device or system may result in compromise of your work credentials, work accounts, or work data. If you suspect your work credentials may have been compromised, you should plan to change those credentials, and report the incident to your employer. If you routinely connect your home system to a work network using a virtual private network (VPN), the possibilities become much more serious, as your home compromise may have "jumped the gap" into your employer's network.

To understand how a cyber incident may affect your work and your workplace, you should consider the following factors:

- **Your work may be the actual target.** You may have been breached at home, but your work may be the actual target. In this day of social media, attackers can correlate databases to match up your personal identities with your professional identities. Attackers may have targeted you at home because it is easier than hacking your workplace and gives them a "back door" into your workplace accounts and networks. Think about what you do professionally and how it might be a target for attackers.
- **Resetting your work credentials.** Along with resetting your personal account credentials, you should consider resetting your work credentials, if you believe they may have been compromised. Note that password reset mechanisms on work networks are usually different from those used for your personal accounts. If you are locked out of your work accounts, you may need to contact your IT help desk or human resources for assistance.
- **Time frame of the compromise.** Think through when your system may have been compromised and what has happened since then. When did you first detect that something was wrong? When was the earliest time you may have been compromised? When was the most likely time that you were compromised? Have you used your work accounts, credentials, network connections, or files since then? If so, do you remember when? What work projects were you working on? What sensitive or customer data did you access? When did you start taking actions to address the problem? What actions did you take? This information will be important if an investigation needs to be conducted.
- **Alerting your security office.** If you suspect your work accounts, credentials, network connections, or files may have been compromised, you should probably alert your employer's security office, along with your management. While this notification can be uncomfortable, it is better than your employer detecting the breach on their own and confronting you. Your employer's secu-

rity office will likely want to start an investigation to understand the possible scope of the compromise and potential damage. To do this investigation, the security office will most likely work with IT and cybersecurity to check logs of when your accounts were used and what files and data attackers may have accessed.

- **Contract and regulatory requirements.** Depending on your employment and your employer's business relationships, compromise related to your account could have contract and/or regulatory consequences. For example, if you are in the medical industry, a compromise could have consequences under the Health Insurance Portability and Accountability Act (HIPAA). If your account has access to customer data and there is evidence of inappropriate access, then your customer contracts may require that they be notified. Your security office's investigation will most likely consider these types of factors. Consider your contracts and business relationships, and their potential regulatory consequences.

- **Possible breaches of data.** Unfortunately, in today's hyper-connected world, even "unimportant" accounts and connections may turn out to be avenues for a breach. The Target Corporation breach of millions of credit cards started from an air conditioning contractor who had access to the Target network. Do you really know everything you have access to at your workplace? Unfortunately, it may be far more than you think. If you are compromised, work with investigators to fully understand the scope and impact of the compromise and any associated data breach.

Understanding the Risks of Being Paperless

It is helpful to remember just how fragile your digital life really is. A hundred years ago our lives revolved around a community of neighbors who knew us and could vouch for us in the business we conducted. Fifty years ago, our lives revolved around the cities and towns where our business was conducted in person with the shops and businesses nearby. Twenty years ago, our lives revolved around our neighborhood, but also a network of nationwide businesses we only knew through accounts, mailing addresses, and telephone numbers. Today our lives revolve around a digital web of online accounts, identities, usernames, and passwords. If those digital identities are lost, our digital life can be lost, as well.

To understand the risks that come with a fully digital life and online accounts, you should consider the following:

- **You could die.** The reality for all of us is that horrible accidents happen every day, and take away people in the prime of their lives. These accidents include parents, siblings, and caregivers upon whom others are dependent. If you die, all of your accounts and passwords go with you, unless they are written down somewhere and someone else can find them. As morbid as this thought is, think it through and consider your successors and beneficiaries.
- **Paperless makes it difficult for survivors.** When you are paperless, your survivors (or helpers if you are merely disabled) have little insight to your digital life. They may have your mobile phone, your computer, and your e-mail addresses, but these devices may all be locked with passcodes they do not know. You need to think through what they will want to know to be able to access your accounts, money, and correspondence to take over handling of your affairs.
- **Consider what is critical.** When was the last time you wrote a letter? For most of us, our personal correspondence is all purely digital. When those digital accounts are lost, all that correspondence is lost as well. The same goes for photographs, videos, and personal documents. Think about what of your accounts and data are most critical, and how others might get to them if you are not there to help.
- **Have records of your most important files and accounts.** For your most important files and accounts, establish some paper records that could be used to get started. A list of your financial accounts and assets is hugely helpful. Also, a list of bills that are configured for e-payment, or that require you to approve e-payment online are helpful. If someone has to take over for you, past due bills and rent or mortgage payments can add up quickly, especially if your income is disrupted at the same time (which it most likely will be).
- **Leave instructions.** Have instructions on what to do in the event of your incapacitation, and make sure those instructions are in the hands of loved ones and trusted friends. Those instructions should include information like points of contact, locations of assets, lists of bills, online accounts, locations of safety deposit boxes, and points of contacts for friends and family. It may only take a couple of pages, but those pages will be invaluable if things go horribly wrong.

Chapter 12
Considering Cybersecurity at Work

The other chapters of this book primarily discuss personal cybersecurity. We have examined how you can protect your personal computers, devices, accounts, and networks from cyber harm. These good practices help to protect your home IT environment, and protect you, your friends, and your family members online. However, although good practices at home can help to reduce your risk at work, such practices are only one part of the cyber defenses you may have at your workplace.

Work computer networks are becoming increasingly complicated, with large numbers of network-connected devices, cloud-base services, and connections to third-party partners, customers, and vendors. As shown in Figure 12.1, work computer networks typically consist of an enterprise network infrastructure that includes: (1) internet connectivity, (2) Wi-Fi connectivity, (3) work functions, and (4) internal and external network infrastructures.

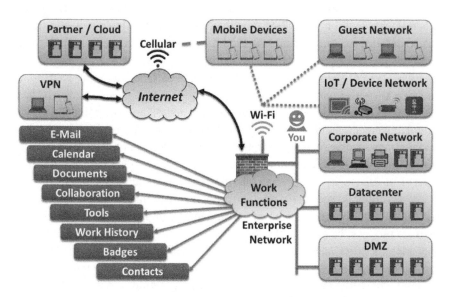

Figure 12.1: Work computer networks are increasingly capable and complex due to technology advancements.

In a workplace environment, good personal cybersecurity practices are combined with enterprise cyber defenses to protect hundreds or thousands of employees

DOI 10.1515/9781501506505-012

who may be working with data that is sensitive, regulated, or even classified. In your workplace, you are participating in a larger cyber defense program that includes additional layers of defenses for prevention, detection, and incident response. These defenses work together to protect you and your coworkers from sophisticated professional cyberattacks.

This chapter describes some of the cybersecurity you can expect to encounter in an enterprise. This chapter does not include *all* enterprise cybersecurity capabilities; rather, it focuses on the capabilities you are most likely to come across as an employee. This chapter provides security awareness tips and best practices to consider when you are operating IT systems in your workplace. The material presented here is offered as guidance that you should consider to be complementary to your enterprise's actual cybersecurity policies, procedures, standards, and guidelines.

Enterprise Cybersecurity Differences

When a person moves from a personal cybersecurity setting to an enterprise cybersecurity environment, there may be a significant difference in the threat levels. Enterprises routinely must defend themselves against professional cybercriminals, skilled hacktivists, and nation-state attackers. While these attackers may use some of the same tools and techniques as those targeting your home network, they also may use advanced techniques. These advanced cyberattack techniques can include: advanced malware, command and control, persistence, lateral movement, and privilege escalation within target IT environments. Professional attackers may turn their targets' IT environment against themselves, and can achieve devastating results affecting tens of thousands of employees, millions of customers, and disrupting billions of dollars in business.

In addition, commercial and enterprise IT environments may be subject to regulatory and other requirements requiring more comprehensive cyber defenses than are practical in a personal or home network. These regulatory requirements may include strict specifications for cyber defense activities regarding identity management, endpoint protection (protection of personal computers and devices), the network perimeter, and incident detection and response. While headlines show these defenses are hardly perfect, they do act to reduce risk and increase the chances cyberattacks will be disrupted, delayed, detected, or defeated before they can do significant damage.

Some of the regulations and standards enterprise IT environments may be subject to include the following:

- **General Data Protection Regulation (GDPR).** This European Union (EU) regulation took effect in 2018 and provides extensive online privacy protection for EU citizens regarding their personal data. GDPR includes significant fines in the event of noncompliance or breaches.
- **Health Insurance Portability and Accountability Act (HIPAA).** This U.S. law passed in 1996 establishes a concept of personal health information (PHI). The law requires that IT security controls be implemented when handling PHI data processed by electronic health records (EHR) medical systems.
- **International Organization for Standardization (ISO) 27001.** This standard from the ISO was first published in 1995 and provides a framework for establishing and assessing an organizational cybersecurity program. As an international standard, it is used by organizations around the world.
- **National Institute for Standards and Technologies (NIST) Cyber Security Framework (CSF).** This standard, from the U.S. NIST, was released in 2014 and is widely used for cybersecurity program organization and assessment in the United States.
- **Payment Card Industry Data Security Standard (PCI DSS).** This standard was first released in 2004, with the intent to standardize cybersecurity protection of payment card (credit card) data stored by merchants and processors.
- **Sarbanes-Oxley Act (SOX).** This U.S. federal law was passed in 2002 and requires strict financial accounting controls for public companies, including cybersecurity. Similar laws have been adopted in many countries including Germany, France, and Japan.

Enterprise Network Perimeter and Security

One of the similarities between a typical enterprise network and a home network is the presence of an internet connection with routers and firewalls. You have these same capabilities at home, albeit usually on a smaller scale. Enterprise internet connections typically include several additional network security capabilities, used to protect the enterprise's internal network and its devices. These security capabilities provide for high-performance filtering of network traffic as well as detection, investigation, and response to cybersecurity incidents.

Enterprises typically use some or all of the following capabilities for network perimeter and security:
- **Firewalls.** This technology provides network filtering at the perimeter and establishes boundaries—on the outside of the network—designed to keep

intruders out. Enterprises may also have firewalls inside the network to separate manufacturing plants from administrative networks, or internet-facing servers from the datacenter. These firewalls may also perform advanced functions like filtering web traffic, authorizing network connections, and detecting cyberattacks.

– **Guest networks.** Enterprise networks typically perform official business only. Allowing guest devices to connect to these "internal" networks may pose an unacceptable risk. To address this problem, enterprises set up "guest" networks to give visitors internet connectivity, while isolating them from the enterprise's internal networks and devices. These guest networks may be wired or wireless but should be clearly marked. They may be password-protected, requiring the "guest" to get "the password of the day" to authorize access. Guest networks are typically segregated to provide only internet connectivity, and do not provide connectivity to internal resources like applications or printers. You should make sure that guests connect to the appropriate guest networks and are properly authorized.

– **Packet Capture Intrusion Detection and Prevention Systems (IDS/IPS).** This technology filters network traffic for the enterprise and can detect (and block) potentially malicious network traffic. Packet capture further improves security by allowing cyber defenders to "replay" suspicious traffic to understand what happened. These systems are usually configured to catch typical cyberattacker activity and command-and-control patterns.

– **Secure Wi-Fi.** Many enterprises also have wireless networking installed. Wi-Fi makes it convenient for employees with mobile devices and laptop computers to get network connectivity. Wi-Fi may also be used for plant or medical networks, enabling mobile and movable equipment to stay connected while moving around the facility. Enterprise Wi-Fi networks typically have stronger protection than home networks, with passwords that change frequently, or requiring tokens or certificates to connect.

Endpoint Hardening and Encryption

In addition to locked-down networks, enterprises typically have "locked down" or "hardened" endpoint computers and devices as well. For personal computers, your enterprise-issued system may be configured to limit your ability to customize or change your system, and to provide protection for the system against common cyberattack techniques. These measures are for your protection and to help enterprise IT personnel manage large numbers of desktop, laptop, and server computers. Hardening involves configuring systems with security policies, antimalware software, and other tools to reduce vulnerabilities and make the systems less susceptible to cyberattack. By hardening endpoints, the enterprise makes it less likely for systems to become compromised, increases its ability to respond to compromise, and protects its data stored on those endpoint systems.

Enterprises typically use some or all the following capabilities for endpoint hardening and encryption:

- **Endpoint management.** By centrally managing endpoint computers and devices, the enterprise can maintain inventory and asset control of its equipment and can also centrally oversee what software is installed and running on enterprise endpoints. This management can be important for software license compliance, and ensuring systems comply with enterprise policies or regulatory requirements. You should be aware if your endpoints are centrally managed, and comply with instructions when, for example, software or patches are delivered to your endpoints for installation.

- **Endpoint hardening and monitoring.** When endpoints are centrally managed, they will likely be configured to make them resistant to cyberattack. Endpoint computers will likely be configured with antimalware tools, network firewalls, data leakage protection, and web and e-mail screening. Endpoint agents may monitor user activity and send alerts of suspicious behavior to central administration consoles. You should be aware of the protections installed on your endpoints and the alerts those protections may display as you use them.

- **Full disk and media encryption.** Data stored on endpoints and mobile devices may also be protected using encryption. This protection may include full-disk encryption for laptop or desktop computer hard drives as well as removable media encryption for external hard drives and thumb drives. Whereas at home these capabilities are usually optional, in the enterprise they may be required for regulatory compliance. This type of encryption can be a significant protection for the enterprise when laptops or removable drives containing sensitive or regulated data are lost or stolen. Because the data is encrypted, the enterprise may not have to report the incident to regulators or publicly announce a data breach. You should be aware of your enterprise's policies for disk and media encryption and comply with them. This awareness is especially important if you handle sensitive or regulated data in your professional duties.

- **Data classification and data loss protection (DLP)**. In addition to hardening endpoints, enterprises may also use data classification and DLP software to keep track of what types of data are stored on endpoint systems, and to detect when sensitive data is sent in or out of the enterprise. These technologies may require you to label documents and e-mail messages you create with appropriate "tags" indicating the type of data they contain. In addition, documents and messages containing data that matches certain templates— like customer account numbers or social security numbers—may be automatically detected and flagged. You should be aware of your enterprise's policies regarding data classification and protection, as well as its regulatory obligations regarding identifying and protecting sensitive data.

Identity and Access Management

A big area of difference between home and enterprise networks has to do with accounts and identity management. In the enterprise, you may have one or more accounts you use to access enterprise applications and resources. These accounts may be used to logon to your enterprise e-mail, collaboration tools, plant equipment, or benefits systems. Your permissions within the enterprise are usually limited by access controls tied to your role or the systems you use. You are assigned permissions that allow you to see the information you need and do the tasks you need to perform, while denying you access to those you do not need.

Enterprises typically use some or all the following capabilities for identity and access management:

- **Enterprise accounts.** Enterprises typically establish "standard" accounts for employees, and may also establish accounts for contractors, partners, and customers. For employees, these accounts are often established when an employee is hired and removed when an employee leaves. Accounts are frequently tied to an e-mail address and protected by a password but may use multifactor authentication as well. You should understand the accounts issued to you, your responsibilities to protect those accounts, and report if you suspect your accounts have been compromised or abused. You should never share your work accounts with others, except as directed by your enterprise.
- **Roles, access control privileges, and periodic recertification.** When employees get enterprise accounts, they frequently get a basic set of privileges, like being able to logon to enterprise computers and e-mail accounts. Additional privileges beyond those may require special approvals and provisioning. Enterprises may establish roles for specific duties like customer support or engineering, with the roles enabling sets of privileges to access systems and applications. In addition, privileges may need to be recertified periodically—say annually—to make sure you still need the privileges assigned to you and to remove them when you no longer need them. You

should be aware of the roles and privileges assigned to you, and your responsibilities for protecting those roles and associated privileges.

- **Accounts for third-party services.** Many enterprises use third-party "cloud" services for supporting business functions such as e-mail, sales tracking, human resources, benefits, or payroll. These services may use your standard enterprise account or may require you to establish a separate account (frequently it is your business e-mail account) for access. Unfortunately, with large numbers of corporate services this approach can result in many accounts and passwords you must manage. You should treat your third-party service accounts like your enterprise accounts and take care to protect them. Be especially careful with benefits and payroll accounts, as attackers who can steal these credentials may be able to intercept your paychecks or benefit payments.

- **Authentication gateways, federation, and single-sign-on (SSO).** To reduce the challenges and risks of employees having multiple accounts for enterprise, third-party, and other services, IT may enable you to logon once—usually through a central website—to get to other enterprise services without needing additional usernames and passwords. These capabilities are powerful and significantly improve employee experiences when there are large numbers of enterprise services. The tradeoff of this approach is that it places even more importance on the security of the employee's main account and its credentials. If your enterprise uses single sign on (SSO), you should be extra careful with your employee credentials and be vigilant for potential signs of compromise.

- **Privileged accounts.** These are special accounts that can deploy or reconfigure IT systems, applications, or data. Privileged accounts may be required to access regulated or classified data not normally available to employees. Because of data sensitivity, enterprises may use password rotation or multifactor authentication to give privileged accounts additional protection from potential compromise. If you are issued a privileged account, you should understand your responsibilities associated with that account, as well as reporting requirements if you believe the account has been compromised or abused.

Web and E-Mail Protection

Enterprises typically provide additional protection for your e-mail and web browsing than you might have at home. This protection may only be available when you are in the office connected to the enterprise network or it may be provided all the time through internet-based "always-on" network connections such as a VPN. In addition, some web filtering can "look inside" secure HTTPS (also known as hypertext transmission protocol secure) connections, permitting examination of secure network traffic to detect malicious activity, malware downloads, data exfiltration, or command and control traffic. The purpose of these protections is to reduce the chance your work computer or device will be compromised by a malicious website, e-mail, or attachment. These protections may also be required to comply with regulatory requirements.

Enterprises typically use some or all of the following capabilities for web and e-mail protection:

- **E-mail filtering, phishing, and spear phishing defenses.** These protections will usually reduce the amount of "spam" or other unwanted mail, malicious attachments, and major phishing and spear phishing campaigns. Studies have found that more than 90% of e-mail transiting the internet is unwanted, so these filters have a lot of work to do. Advanced phishing can be very difficult to block, so do not expect that e-mail filtering will protect you from *all* potentially malicious e-mail. However, it should reduce your risk. In addition, e-mail filtering may work with web filtering to further protect you if you should click on a link in a malicious message and get directed to a malicious website. Note that your protections may be different when you are in an enterprise facility connected to the enterprise network, versus when you are outside the enterprise network or on a home network. You should be aware of what e-mail protection is in place at your enterprise, and how it can and can not protect you from potentially malicious e-mail.

- **E-mail nonrepudiation and encryption.** As has been previously discussed, e-mail is notoriously insecure and advanced attackers can easily generate fraudulent and counterfeit e-mails that are difficult or even impossible to distinguish from legitimate messages. If you are involved in customer service sending e-mail messages to customers, you must deal with these challenges in your communications. These challenges include transmitting sensitive, confidential, or protected customer information, such as data for customers' health care, accounts, or finances. To protect these transmissions, your enterprise may employ *secure e-mail* technologies that provide for *nonrepudiation* and *encryption* of sensitive messages. Nonrepudiation proves your e-mail message came from you or your organization and is legitimate. Encryption protects sensitive data in your message from being read by others as it transits the internet. You should understand what e-mail security features are available at your enterprise, and when and how you should use them to reduce your organization's liability and potential exposure due to data breaches.

- **Web filtering and decryption.** These protections involve intercepting web browsing network traffic from enterprise computers and scanning that traffic for potentially malicious patterns. This filtering may include blocking certain websites, like social media or pornography. It may also include watching web traffic for data patterns like command and control signals, or transmission of large data files like databases or proprietary data. Filtering may be able to look inside encrypted web traffic (using https:// web addresses) and view private transmissions including passwords. Web filtering generally requires you to be connected to an enterprise network from an enterprise facility, but may apply to remote access as well. You should be aware of what web filtering policies exist at your enterprise, make sure you do not visit inappropriate websites, and understand how web filtering may protect you from malicious websites.

Remote Access to Enterprise IT Resources

For many employees, remote access to enterprise IT resources is critically important. While on the road, sales personnel need to be able to pull up materials and customer status, consultants need to be able to access reference materials, and mobile repair teams need to be able to connect to back-end databases. More and more personnel are working from home offices or customer locations. These employees need to have the same functionality from a laptop computer or a mobile device as they would have if they were in an office building at a desktop terminal. To support these requirements, enterprises deploy remote access solutions. Remote access may be as simple as internet-based access to e-mail or it may be elaborate virtual private network (VPN) connections. Remote access technologies may support employees on the road, employees working from home, and employees using bring your own device (BYOD) and mobile device management (MDM).

Enterprises typically use some or all the following capabilities for remote access to enterprise IT resources:
- **Multifactor authentication.** Whenever enterprises make sensitive IT resources available over the internet, it is prudent to use some sort of multifactor authentication to protect those resources. Multifactor authentication uses additional factors—like a card, token, device, or biometric—to positively identify you when you connect to enterprise resources. These additional factors make it considerably more difficult for attackers who obtain your username and password to impersonate you from the internet. You may be

required to use multifactor authentication for secure remote access to your enterprise, and should follow the procedures for the technology being used.

- **VPN.** The simplest form of remote access is VPN, which uses a secure network "tunnel" to connect securely your computer into the enterprise's internal network. A VPN can give you complete access to the enterprise network, as if you were sitting on a computer inside the office or headquarters facility. But this power brings risks, as it also means malware on your computer could also be given access to the network. To guard against this risk, VPN connections may include firewalls and network monitoring. You should be aware of the VPN policy at your enterprise and ensure you only VPN using authorized devices and under appropriate circumstances. You should be extra cautious with VPN when the computer you are using is trusted for sensitive operations, or is a personal system that is only lightly protected.

- **Virtual desktop.** To reduce the risk of employees connecting personal computers to enterprise networks using VPN, many enterprises deploy virtual desktop technology. This technology gives you a "virtual desktop" connection to a computer that is installed at the enterprise datacenter, using a web browser window or a custom client installed on your computer or device. The advantage of this approach is you get a complete enterprise desktop experience with the appropriate security measures in place. It also makes it more difficult for malware on your personal computer to "jump the gap" and attack the enterprise's network. When using virtual desktop, you should be aware of the capabilities and limitations of the desktop environment and understand how you are to do common activities like exporting files or printing documents.

- **Internet-facing applications**. In addition to VPN and virtual desktop, many enterprises make productivity applications *internet-facing*. These applications may include e-mail, collaboration, file transfer, service requests, sales tracking, human resources, or benefits. The enterprise may protect these applications with multifactor authentication or may make them available using simple usernames and passwords. When using internet-facing enterprise applications, you should make sure you are on a trusted computer or an enterprise device. If on a personal device, you should take care with what data you are accessing, and make sure you are not downloading or uploading controlled or proprietary data that should not be leaving the enterprise.

- **Bring your own device (BYOD) and mobile device management (MDM).** To reduce costs and improve employee experiences, many enterprises have policies for BYOD and MDM. BYOD involves allowing employees to access enterprise resources using their own personal computers and mobile devices. BYOD may even involve allowing employees to buy their own computing equipment and use it for organizational purposes. When employees use personal mobile devices, enterprises may use MDM to create a secure "bubble" on those devices where enterprise data resides. This secured area is encrypted on the device and remotely managed by the enterprise, including the ability to remotely delete it. Enterprise data—like e-mail and documents—stays within the secured area for protection. If your enterprise has policies for BYOD and/or MDM, you should consider these policies and the benefits and challenges of using your own devices for company business, especially if the work you are doing is regulated. You should make sure your device and its configuration comply with enterprise policies, and report if you have concerns that your personal system may have been compromised with malware.

Personnel Cybersecurity Training

Any time an enterprise needs its employees' cooperation to achieve success, training is going to be of paramount importance. For cybersecurity, enterprises typically have some level of basic cybersecurity training that is conducted periodically (typically once a year). They may also have more involved training for personnel who are in positions of trust or sensitivity, like executives and systems administrators. In addition, personnel who are engaged in regulated activity or handling regulated data may require additional training on regulatory requirements. Cybersecurity training may be standalone training, or it may be integrated with other training on general security practices, business risk, or regulatory compliance. This training is important to help employees be aware of the organization's cyber risks, how the organization can mitigate those risks, and the employees' responsibilities regarding those mitigations.

Enterprises typically use some or all the following approaches for personnel security training:
- **Regular security awareness training.** The foundation of employee cybersecurity training is for the enterprise to implement regular security awareness training and testing for company personnel. This training may include information on company security policy, evolving security threats, online scams, and IT basics regarding e-mail, social media, and collaboration tool usage. Training may also be required for contractors and partners who have access to enterprise IT systems. You should be aware of this training, take it seriously, and apply its guidance in your day-to-day work.
- **Phishing tests and training.** Phishing and spear phishing are the two most common ways cyberattackers get into enterprise IT environments today.

Attackers may phish or spear phish employees directly, or they may get in through indirect means like a trusted partner or a VPN connection. As part of ongoing security awareness, many enterprises engage services to actively "phish" their employees. This mock phishing identifies those who are susceptible to real-world phishing and provides them with additional training on how to recognize and avoid being phished for real. You should watch out for phishing e-mails at all times and understand that some of them may be for training. Forward phishing messages to your cybersecurity department for follow-up.

- **Executive and systems administrator training.** Executives and systems administrators often have access to privileged and regulated information that is far more sensitive than what is seen by the typical employee. Compromise of one of their computers or accounts can have dire consequences including draining of company bank accounts or widespread destruction of company IT systems. Consequently, these personnel may receive additional training on cyberthreats and defenses against advanced attacks. If you are an executive or a systems administrator, you should be aware of the risks associated with your role, and the additional protections being applied to you, your computers, and your enterprise accounts.

Cybersecurity Operations and Incident Response

Another area where enterprise environments are significantly different from a home network is security operations. For an enterprise, occasionally checking logs is not enough to protect hundreds or thousands of employees, contractors, partners, and customers. Enterprises need 24×7 monitoring of their IT environment to detect potentially malicious activity, investigate that activity, and respond to malicious cyber incidents. These activities fall under the umbrella of *cybersecurity operations* and are an important part of an enterprise's overall cyber defense posture. Larger enterprises are going to be occasionally breached, one way or another. What is most important is not their resistance to being breached in the first place, but their ability to detect and respond to the breach after it has started, but before significant damage can been done.

Enterprises typically use some or all the following capabilities for cybersecurity operations and incident response:
- **Cybersecurity monitoring.** Incident detection starts with monitoring of the enterprise's IT environment and its cyber defenses. Monitoring detects signs of malware, malicious network activity, malicious application activity,

and malicious account activity when they occur within the enterprise. Monitoring does this detection by tying together sensors across the enterprise network, perimeter, filters, applications, and endpoints, and then feeding those sensors into engines that analyze and correlate detected events. You should be aware that everything you do on your enterprise IT systems may be monitored, and careless or malicious activity may raise alerts trigging an investigation.

– **Cyber incident detection and investigation.** Once the enterprise establishes security monitoring of its cyber defenses and other IT systems, it must establish criteria for incident detection and investigation. Network perimeters can generate thousands or even millions of events every day, most of which are of little consequence. Enterprises must "tune" their monitoring systems to identify real security incidents and investigate those incidents to find cyberintruders. This investigation involves identifying computers, accounts, and network addresses involved in malicious activity. You should be aware that your enterprise may have to investigate cyber incidents related to you, your accounts, your computer, or your colleagues. When such investigations occur, you will be expected to cooperate with investigators, which may include not using your accounts or devices for some period of time.

– **Cyber incident response.** When the enterprise identifies real cyber intrusions, it may find itself in a dangerous game of "cat and mouse" with the intruders. Professional cyber intruders can gain access to enterprises for days or months before finally triggering a massive data breach. This time may be required for them to find the data they are interested in, get access to computers hosting that data, and obtain user credentials with the privileges to access that data. When defenders discover an intrusion is in progress, attackers may have access to dozens of computers and accounts within the enterprise, which makes "kicking them out" extremely difficult. Cyber incident response involves repelling cyberintruders in such a way that it will be hard for them to get back in again. You should understand the seriousness and difficulty of incident response. And any cyber-response activities that involve you require your full cooperation and attention.

Physical Security and Personnel Protection

Physical security and protection of personnel are critical elements of a successful enterprise security program. Protection of logical data starts with protection of the physical location and media where that data resides, and may include encrypting data to reduce the risk of physical compromise. Similarly, cybersecurity must take into account the people who can access enterprise data, and the trustworthiness of the personnel. Physical and personnel protection frequently involve coordination between cybersecurity and industrial security departments of the enterprise. Your enterprise's programs may include some of these coordination points, and they may be reflected in the organization's policies, procedures, and training.

Enterprise physical security and personnel protection programs typically include the following elements:

- **Facility and personnel protection.** Enterprise physical security and personnel protection programs might include door locks, alarm systems, security guards, and law enforcement liaisons. Personnel protection may include access badges, restricted areas, security screening, and metal detectors. Many enterprises are weapon- and drug-free zones, subject to local laws and regulations. You should be aware of the facility and personnel policies in place at your enterprise, take them seriously, and be cognizant of suspicious activity like strangers wandering around or propped-opened doors.

- **Personnel security, background checks, and drug screening.** Employee security and trust is an important part of enterprise protection, especially when sensitive or regulated data is being handled. Malicious or negligent employees or other insiders can cause immeasurable and irreparable harm when things go wrong. Regulations may require significant background checks, including drug screening for certain positions of trust or public safety. Enterprises may establish their own policies that exceed regulatory requirements, for many of the same reasons. You should be aware of the personnel security requirements at your enterprise, including requirements for background checks and/or drug screening. You should remember this trust is not just a one-time event and criminal activity during your employment may become grounds for dismissal.

- **Security incident reporting.** Any time an organization has a security program, there will also be security incident detection, investigation, and reporting. The organization may be required to perform certain incident handling for regulatory compliance. Also, the organization or the security office may do these activities to meet other business objectives like reducing theft losses, crime prevention, or protecting the safety of employees, customers, or guests. As a part of incident reporting, employees may be required to report certain types of security incidents, including suspected criminal activity. This reporting may include personal events like international travel, criminal arrests, or workplace accidents. You should be aware of your enterprise's policies regarding security activities, and be vigilant toward looking after everyone's safety and security.

Business Continuity and Disaster Recovery

Just as with protecting your home IT environment, business continuity and disaster recovery is of paramount importance to the enterprise. Disasters can occur for many reasons—not just those caused by cyberattacks—and the business must be able to continue in the face of considerable adversity or other challenges. Most enterprises do considerable planning for how the business might continue in the face of natural, man-made, or criminal disaster situations. For IT and cyber, these efforts revolve around responding to and recovering from significant IT failures and cyberattacks, including enterprise-wide outages, large-scale malware outbreaks, and ransomware holding the enterprise hostage.

Enterprise business continuity and disaster recovery efforts typically include the following capabilities:
- **Enterprise backup.** Just as with your home network, backups are the foundation of business continuity and disaster recovery. If the enterprise can not recover its computers, accounts, applications, and data, it will have nothing after a disaster occurs. Enterprise backup typically includes additional features beyond a typical home backup, such as backup of individual personal computers, backup of servers, databases, and enterprise data, and large-scale "bare metal" backup of enterprise servers and infrastructure. You should be aware of how enterprise backup works at your enterprise, including if any of the systems you normally use are *not* regularly backed up. If your personal computers are not backed up, you should think about what your contingency plans would be if your main computer were lost, stolen, or suffered a hardware failure. If you back up your work computer yourself, make sure your backups are protected with appropriate encryption and physical protection.
- **Contingency planning.** Your enterprise will likely do contingency planning for various adversity scenarios. These scenarios might include natural or man-made disasters, loss of facilities, loss of personnel, or loss of connectivity. Some situations—like the failure of a third party—may be handled more gracefully than others. Many scenarios may have adverse effect on the organization's reputation or long-term impacts on its business. Many contingency plans have to do with keeping the most critical operational systems online even when things go wrong, while simultaneously dealing with the underlying problems and protecting the enterprise's people. You should be aware of your enterprise's contingency plans and how it intends to communicate with employees, partners, and customers in the event of a crisis. You should understand your responsibilities in the event of a crisis, and what you

should do if personnel, facilities, and/or online systems are impaired or not available.

– **IT disaster recovery.** The final component of business continuity and disaster recovery has to do with recovery of IT systems. Enterprise disaster recovery planning should include plans to restore data and business applications after a "disaster" that might involve the dramatic loss of facilities, personnel, or significant impairment of IT systems and services. These disasters may be natural—such as hurricanes or earthquakes—or they may be man-made—such as power outages, espionage, sabotage, violent crime, or warfare. You should be aware of how your enterprise may act to restore its services in a disaster recovery situation, as is appropriate to your role. You should understand your responsibilities in a disaster situation, where you should go, the actions you should take, and the people with whom you should coordinate, so you can be a part of the solution in a difficult situation.

Chapter 13
Final Thoughts

Over the past twelve chapters, we have talked about your digital life, the threats against it, and some techniques for protecting it against today's cyber threats. Modern IT is dizzyingly complex, with the average household containing dozens of times the computing power that put people on the moon two generations ago. With this technology, we can record and share our digital lives in ways never before possible, and access our lives' data at a moment's notice, all while on the go. It truly is remarkable what we can do. Some would argue that the digital revolution is just getting started, with the best yet to come.

Yet these capabilities come with risks attached to them. As authors and Hollywood have speculated, digital lives can be disrupted just as easily as they can be created, and cleaning up the mess of a hack or a compromise can be disruptive, time consuming, and disconcerting. This journey to a digital future is just beginning, and many security growing pains may remain before it is really secure *and* convenient, all at the same time.

In the future, cyberattacks may become much faster more devastating (and potentially deadlier), than they have been in the past. As more and more capabilities are network-connected—including infrastructure like cars, roads, electricity, and water—it may become possible for cyberattackers to disrupt more than just our e-mail or web browsing. A dangerous cat-and-mouse game is going to take place as engineers learn to leverage the capability of the network for new functions and functionalities, and attackers learn how to target those capabilities and functions for potential harm. An arms race between cyber innovators and cyberattackers is inevitable until some type of relatively safe "balance" is established. Until we achieve this "future digital nirvana," we are stuck with the present reality of a patchwork of computers, phones, tablets, peripherals, smart devices, usernames, and passwords we have to manage and secure by hand. It isn't pretty, but like so many things in life, it can be made to work well enough.

In this book, we have attempted to provide you with some tools and techniques you can use to secure your own digital life, as it exists today. While we know the technologies will continue to evolve at a breakneck pace, we hope the principles of good cybersecurity, and the techniques we are sharing with you for implementing these principles, will endure.

DOI 10.1515/9781501506505-013

Appendix A
Common Online Scams

Malicious e-mails and websites may work together, along with telephone calls or call centers, to implement elaborate online scams. These scams are usually financial in nature, seeking to generate fraudulent charges, obtain online credentials or bank access, or to get victims to pay for help they really do not need.

This appendix describes some typical characteristics of malicious e-mails and some of the more popular online scams. These descriptions are just a selection of online scams. Search the internet for "common internet scams" to find information on dozens of scams that are occurring every day.

Common Characteristics of Phishing E-Mails

Phishing and spear phishing e-mails are messages designed with the goal of getting the recipient to do something. Most often, these scams involve getting the victim to install a program, open a document, or visit a website. The program, document, or website are in turn malicious and designed to take control of the victim's computer or steal their credentials. Figure A.1 depicts an example of a phishing e-mail.

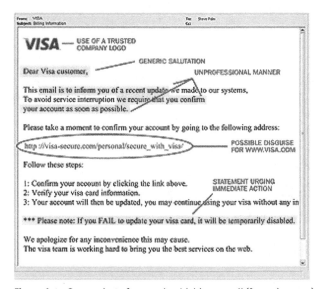

Figure A.1: Screenshot of a sample phishing e-mail (from visa.com).

DOI 10.1515/9781501506505-014

Some characteristics of phishing and malicious e-mails include the following:
- E-mail address (user@domain.com) is invalid.
- Salutation is unusual, generic, or missing.
- Text contains typos, poor wording, or unprofessional language.
- Message contains an offer that is too good to be true.
- Message urges immediate action and threatens consequences for inaction.
- Message asks you to click on a link in the message to login to your account.
- Signature is unusual or missing.
- Business e-mail lacks legal language in the footer, or "unsubscribe" links.
- Attachments don't match the content of the message.
- Attachments have generic names, like "invoice.pdf."
- When opened, the attachment is blank.
- Links do not go to recognizable addresses.
- Links take you to sites that ask you to logon but do not look like normal websites.

Spear phishing e-mails may appear to come from someone you know and may be backed up by sophisticated attackers. If you respond to the e-mail, attackers may even reply to you telling you the message is legitimate and the link or attachment is okay to open.

Common Subject Lines for Malicious E-Mails

Another characteristic of phishing e-mails—particularly untargeted ones sent to thousands or millions of people—is that subject lines are often inconsistent with legitimate personal or business purposes. The following list contains some subject lines that are frequently used for phishing, ransomware, or other online scams *(adapted from CSO Online, Webroot Inc., and KnowBe4)*:
- **Banking and e-commerce**
    - o   Action Required: Pay your account balance
    - o   Amazon: Billing address mismatch
    - o   Deactivation of your account
    - o   Online Banking Alert: Your Account will be Deactivated
    - o   Your recent payment notice
    - o   Wire Transfer
- **Charity, personal, and social**
    - o   Assist Urgently
    - o   Book your vacation!
    - o   Charity Donation for You

- FYI
- Hi
- Remember me from school?
- **Computers and passwords**
  - Change of Password Required Immediately
  - Microsoft: updates to our terms of use
  - Password Check Required Immediately
  - Unauthorized login attempt
  - Unusual sign-in activity
  - Urgent Action Required
- **Employment and IT desk**
  - All Employees: Update your Healthcare Info
  - IT DESK: Reset your password
  - IT DESK: Security alert
  - Please Read: Important from HR
  - Revised Vacation and Sick Time Policy
  - Staff Review
  - Update your direct deposit information
  - Urgent press release to all staff
- **General security and news**
  - BREAKING News
  - Campus Security Notification
  - Security Alert
- **Government**
  - FBI notification
  - Get your tax refund
  - U.S. District Court: Subpoena in a civil case
- **Package delivery**
  - A Delivery Attempt was made
  - FedEx Delivery Attempt
  - USPS: Failed Package Delivery
  - UPS Label Delivery

In addition, scammers may take advantage of current events to target national news, natural disasters, and other timely news that may prod people to action.

Watching Out for Scams and Scam Sites

Scams may bring together e-mail messaging, phony websites, and even telemarketers to target their victims. Scammers are often professional criminals employing teams of people with the sole objective of stealing money from unsuspecting victims. They may make their money by doing any or all of the following:

–   **Getting you to pay them directly.** Scammers may try to get your credit card information or banking information so they can generate charges against you. They may try small charges you are likely to overlook as well as larger charges that make them more money. Once they have your information, they may generate charges until you have the card revoked or the bank account frozen.

–   **Getting you to donate to a phony charity.** Especially in times of crisis, people want to donate. Scammers know you may be inclined to donate to a charity supporting the disaster of the day, even if the "charity" is actually just a criminal front.

–   **Getting you to call toll phone numbers.** Scammers may use toll calls to get you to pay them through your phone company, by calling—or getting transferred to—toll telephone numbers. This scam also works with international calls, which may be even harder for victims to understand and track.

–   **Getting you to give up personal information.** Scammers may get you to give up personal information that allows them to perform identity theft against you and open accounts using your identity and credit rating. They may also sell this information to identity theft rings.

–   **Selling your personal information.** Even if scammers can only confirm your name, address, or phone number, this information is still valuable to aggregators, who pay more for "valid" personal information or information like "will answer the phone" or "is a customer of __ store." These scams may just enable further targeting and potential crime against you, in the future.

Scams take many forms, although they can usually be identified by their goal of making money for the operators. The challenge is it may take some time for you to figure out what the scammers are actually trying to do. The best scammers seek to take advantage of you before you have fully understood what is actually going on.

Some general tips regarding identifying and protecting yourself from scams include the following:

–   **Web browsing.** Use care when "surfing" the web and remember that even major, legitimate websites may be malicious due to malvertising or a temporary cybersecurity incident. Do not search for free versions of commercial software because they are most likely malicious and hosted by malicious sites. The same guidance goes for trying to get free access to copyrighted material like movies, music, or books.

- **Pop-ups and pop-up advertisements.** Be wary of "pop-up" messages that appear over websites you are visiting, or appear on your computer unsolicited. Frequently, these messages are malvertising or other scams intended to dupe unsuspecting users. A popular scam involves encouraging the user to call a "technical support" line. If you should encounter this scam:
    o Do not call the number that pops up on the screen. If you receive an unsolicited call about your computer, know that it is most likely *also* a scam.
    o Only give remote access to your computer to people you know and trust.
    o Never share your password or control of your computer to someone who calls you unsolicited.
    o If a pop-up message appears and will not go away, press Ctrl-Alt-Del (on a PC) to open Task Manager and stop the offending program. You may also need to restart your computer.
    o If the pop-up continues even after restarting, you may need to get technical support to remove the malicious software.

The following sections briefly describe some other common online scams.

Antivirus and Tech Support Scams

The antivirus scam involves convincing the victim their computer has been infected by malware, and they need to install or update "antivirus" software to protect their computer. Usually, this scam is implemented by an aggressive pop-up from a malicious website or malvertisement. The pop-up window may include phony technical details about the "infection," and may also include phone numbers for technical support. Variants of this scam may say the computer needs to be updated, repaired, or otherwise needs technical support service.

At the time the pop-up appears, there is usually nothing wrong with the victim's computer. It is just an aggressive pop-up window using the web browser's built-in windowing functionality to display itself. However, if victims click on the link and install the software, their computers usually become infected with malware that may include backdoors, rootkits, botnet software, or ransomware. Victims who call the technical support number may be talked through the process of installing the malware by a skilled scammer technical support agent. Variants of this scam may also attempt to get the victim to pay for the "technical support" they are receiving, usually in multiple transactions that can add up to hundreds of dollars.

Victims need to make sure they close the pop-ups without clicking anywhere inside them, as the window's content could be malicious and could be attempting to compromise the victim's computer, in addition to trying to scam them. Tech support scammers may also use unsolicited phone calls, claiming that there is a problem with the victim's computer or their software licenses are invalid.

Internal Revenue Service (IRS) Scam

IRS scams are extremely popular around tax time, and focus on capturing personal information, banking information, and online IRS portal information. A frequent objective of these scams is to intercept IRS tax refunds, or get victims to unwittingly give their banking information to the attackers. These scams usually use phishing to direct victims to phony versions of the IRS website, or to get victims to give up their IRS website credentials or banking information.

People who fall victim to these scams may find their IRS refund routed to the scammers' bank instead of their own, or may find funds taken from their personal bank accounts. One version of this scam tells victims they owe the IRS money, and then tries to get the victims to pay the tax to the scammers by giving up their credit card information.

Law Enforcement Scam

Law enforcement scams usually involve an e-mail message threatening the victim with criminal prosecution, or pop-up windows indicating the victim's computer has been involved in criminal activity. Figure A-2 shows an example of one such pop-up window scam, from the U.S. Federal Bureau of Investigation (FBI).

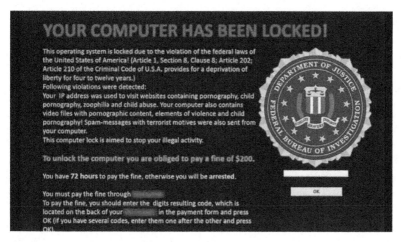

YOUR COMPUTER HAS BEEN LOCKED!

This operating system is locked due to the violation of the federal laws of the United States of America! (Article 1, Section 8, Clause 8; Article 202; Article 210 of the Criminal Code of U.S.A. provides for a deprivation of liberty for four to twelve years.)
Following violations were detected:
Your IP address was used to visit websites containing pornography, child pornography, zoophilia and child abuse. Your computer also contains video files with pornographic content, elements of violence and child pornography! Spam-messages with terrorist motives were also sent from your computer.
This computer lock is aimed to stop your illegal activity.

To unlock the computer you are obliged to pay a fine of $200.

You have 72 hours to pay the fine, otherwise you will be arrested.

You must pay the fine through
To pay the fine, you should enter the digits resulting code, which is located on the back of your ▬▬ in the payment form and press OK (if you have several codes, enter them one after the other and press OK).

Figure A.2: Law enforcement scam pop-up involving the FBI.

If a pop-up window is used, it may be configured to be difficult to close, effectively rendering the victim's computer unusable. Victims who respond to this scam are instructed to pay money or wire money to various locations, or may be convinced to accept "technical support" to fix their computer.

Medicare and Social Security Scams

In 2018, Medicare began transitioning to new Medicare ID cards containing new ID numbers instead of social security numbers. The purpose of these new ID cards is to reduce identity theft based on stolen social security numbers. However, scammers moved quickly to take advantage of this transition to their own benefit. Scammers used telephone calls and e-mails to target victims, telling them they needed to make a payment to get their new ID cards or their Medicare benefits would be suspended. Attackers also attempted to get victims to buy additional Medicare insurance or to give up information that the attackers could use for identity theft, fraudulent medical care, or fraudulent banking transactions.

These scams center around the importance of Medicare and social security numbers that are often used in financial transactions. Scammers try to get this information from unsuspecting (and often tech-un-savvy) seniors, and then use it for fraudulent financial gain. Medical fraud can be particularly difficult to resolve, due to the complexity of medical care and billing processes. By the time the fraudulent transactions are identified, the scammers are long gone.

Natural Disaster and Charity Scams

Natural disaster and charity scams try to get the victims to make "donations" to fake charities, or to legitimate charities that operate with extremely high overheads to enrich their operators while passing on little to the advertised intended beneficiaries. These scams are usually adapted to current news headlines, seeking to support soldiers overseas, local emergency responders, or emergency responses to recent natural disasters. Unfortunately, these scams can be very difficult to identify without conducting a fair amount of research.

To guard against these scams, people should be cautious when donating, and decline to donate when called unsolicited. If the cause seems like a good one, do some research and check with the Federal Trade Commission and Better Business Bureau. Once you have checked the causes and organization out, donate through their website or by calling them. This approach also protects against scammers purporting to be with legitimate charities like the Red Cross, but actually being fraudulent.

Nigerian Prince Scam

This scam is one of the oldest internet scams, and involves the victim receiving an e-mail message asking for help transferring money across international borders. The message usually includes a detailed story stating the sender is a prince, government official, wealthy individual, or some other important person. This "important" person needs help transferring a large sum of money across international borders. In exchange for your assistance, you will be generously compensated.

Victims who "bite" at the scam are sent communications and paperwork to make the scam appear very legitimate. Then, they are asked to pay various fees up-front to help facilitate the transaction. In the end, the victims are bilked out of their own real funds, while never receiving any of the promised scam money.

Appendix B
The Worst Passwords Ever

SplashData (www.teamsid.com) published a list of "the Worst Passwords of 2017." Table B.1 lists SplashData's top twenty worst passwords, but you can see the complete list of 100 passwords at https://www.teamsid.com/worst-passwords-2017-full-list/

Table B.1: SplashData's list of the top twenty worst passwords for 2017.

1.	123456	2.	Password	3.	12345678
4.	Qwerty	5.	12345	6.	123456789
7.	letmein	8.	1234567	9.	football
10.	iloveyou	11.	admin	12.	welcome
13.	monkey	14.	login	15.	abc123
16.	starwars	17.	123123	18.	dragon
19.	passw0rd	20.	master		

Attackers will take lists of passwords like the one shown in Table B-1 and load them into scripts that will try these passwords, one after another, against popular websites. If you use a poor password like one of those on this list, your chances of attackers successfully "guessing" your password are much higher.

Table B.1 passwords aren't the only bad passwords out there, but they are definitely ones to avoid. With a little online searching, you can download lists of 1,000, 10,000, or even a million common passwords. Even uncommon words should be avoided, as it is equally easy to download lists of thousands and thousands of words, in various languages, and then use them to attempt to logon to accounts. As one of their first hacking approaches, attackers will use such password lists to attempt to break into your accounts. Do not be a victim!

DOI 10.1515/9781501506505-015

Appendix C
Online Security Resources

The online resources listed in this appendix are a sample of security references that provide guidance on various security issues in the workplace and home. *The short online resource descriptions provided are quoted or significantly paraphrased from the online resource.*

This resource list is not exhaustive. Most of the entries are resources that the authors reviewed during the preparation of this book, but their review does not constitute their endorsement. These resources are mostly from the United States, but generally apply worldwide.

1. **American Association of Retired Persons (AARP)**
   https://www.aarp.org/
   https://www.aarp.org/money/scams-fraud/info-2018/biggest-frauds-fd.html

   AARP is a United States-based interest group whose stated mission is "empowering people to choose how they live as they age." According to the organization, as of 2018, it had more than 38 million members.

2. **Carnegie Mellon University**
   https://www.sei.cmu.edu/about/divisions/cert/index.cfm

   CERT experts are a diverse group of researchers, software engineers, security analysts, and digital intelligence specialists working together to research security vulnerabilities in software products, contribute to long-term changes in networked systems, and develop cutting-edge information and training to improve the practice of cybersecurity.

   Focus areas include:
   Cyber center development, digital forensics, network situational awareness, system and platform evaluation, cyber intelligence, enterprise risk management, security-aware acquisition, threat-aware sustainment, cyber operator development, insider threat, and secure development.

3. **China Internet Security Law**
   www.china.org.cn/english/China/218754.htm

   State Security Law of the People's Republic of China

DOI 10.1515/9781501506505-001

- Chapter I General Provisions
- Chapter II Functions and Powers of the State Security Organs in the Work of State Security
- Chapter III Duties and Rights of Citizens and Organizations in Safeguarding State Security
- Chapter IV Legal Liability
- Chapter V Supplementary Provisions

4. **CISCO 2018 Annual Cybersecurity Report**
https://www.cisco.com/c/en/us/products/security/security-reports.html

This annual cybersecurity report describes the evolution of malware, malicious encrypted web traffic, and the rise of artificial intelligence. Major findings include:
- "Burst attacks" grow in complexity, frequency, and duration.
- Many new domains tied to spam campaigns.
- Security is seen as a benefit of hosting networks in the cloud.
- Insider threats: A few rogue users can have a big impact.
- More operational technology (OT) and internet of things (IoT) attacks are on the horizon.
- The multivendor environment affects risk.

5. **ConnectSafely**
http://www.connectsafely.org/

ConnectSafely.org is a Silicon Valley, Calif.-based nonprofit organization dedicated to educating users of Smart Connected Things (ScoT) about safety, privacy and security.

6. **Federal Bureau of Investigation**
https://www.fbi.gov/investigate/cyber
https://www.ic3.gov/default.aspx
https://www.fbi.gov/news/stories/2017-internet-crime-report-released-050718
https://www.fbi.gov/scams-and-safety/on-the-internet
- Cyber Crime
The FBI is the lead [United States] federal agency for investigating cyberattacks by criminals, overseas adversaries, and terrorists.
The threat is incredibly serious—and growing. Cyber intrusions are becoming more commonplace, more dangerous, and more sophisticated.

Our nation's critical infrastructure, including both private and public-sector networks, are targeted by adversaries. American companies are targeted for trade secrets and other sensitive corporate data, and universities for their cutting-edge research and development. Citizens are targeted by fraudsters and identity thieves, and children are targeted by online predators.

– Internet Crime Complaint Center (IC3)
   The IC3 accepts online internet crime complaints from either the actual victim or from a third party to the complainant.

– 2017 Internet Crime Report
   The IC3 publishes an annual report detailing victim complaints and disseminates the report to appropriate law enforcement agencies for possible investigation.

   o Scams and safety on the internet include:
      ■ E-scams & warnings
      ■ Internet fraud
      ■ How to protect your computer
      ■ Risk of peer-to-peer systems/networks that allow users connected to the internet to link their computers with other computers around the world.

7. **Federal Trade Commission**
   https://www.consumer.ftc.gov/topics/online-security
   https://www.consumer.ftc.gov/blog/2018/03/top-frauds-2017?utm_source=govdelivery
   https://www.consumer.ftc.gov/articles/0003-phishing
   https://www.ftc.gov/news-events/audio-video/consumers/onguard-online

   – Online-security
      The internet offers access to a world of products and services, entertainment and information. At the same time, it creates opportunities for scammers, hackers, and identity thieves. Learn how to protect your computer, your information, and your online files.

      o Top frauds of 2017
         ■ Debt collection
         ■ Identity theft
            ● Credit card fraud
            ● Tax fraud
      o Imposter scams
         ■ A loved one in trouble
         ■ A government official

- Technical support
- Someone else who is not who they say they are, but who wants your money
  o Travel fraud
  o Vacation fraud
  o Timeshares fraud

– Phishing

Phishing is when a scammer uses fraudulent e-mails or texts, or copycat websites to get you to share valuable personal information—such as account numbers, social security numbers, or your login IDs and passwords. Scammers use your information to steal your money or identity or both.

– OnGuard Online

Site provides a series of short online videos that include the following topics:

  o Hacked E-mail: What to Do
  o Hijacked Computer: What to Do
  o Back It Up: Don't Lose Your Digital Life
  o Computer Security
  o Online Shopping Tips
  o Public Wi-Fi Networks
  o Protect Your Computer from Malware
  o Share with Care
  o Net Cetera: Chatting with Kids About Being Online
  o Phishy Home
  o Phishy Office
  o Phishy Store
  o Stand Up to Cyberbullying
  o The Protection Connection
  o Heads Ups: Stop. Think. Click.

8. **Gov.UK**

https://www.gov.uk/
https://www.gov.uk/search?q=cybersecurity

The websites of all government departments and many other agencies and public bodies have been merged into GOV.UK.

9. **Have I been pwned?**

https://haveibeenpwned.com/

This website checks your e-mail account to determine if it has been compromised in a data breach. The website also provides short descriptions of the largest breaches to include:

- Onliner spambot accounts
- Exploit.In accounts
- Anti-public combo list accounts
- River City media spam list accounts
- MySpace accounts
- NetEase accounts
- LinkedIn accounts
- Adobe accounts
- Exactis accounts
- Apollo accounts

10. **Information is Beautiful**

https://informationisbeautiful.net/

http://www.informationisbeautiful.net/visualizations/worlds-biggest-data-breaches-hacks/

The website visualizes data, information, and knowledge in a number of categories to include the following:

- Living data—world's biggest data breaches & hacks
- Interactive—the internet of things – an interactive primer

11. **National Criminal Justice Reference Center**

https://ncjrs.gov/spotlight/identity_theft/publications.html

- International
- Law enforcement
- Phishing
- Prevention
- Solutions
- Statistics
- Victims

12. **National Cyber-Forensics & Training Alliance**
    https://www.ncfta.net/

    The National Cyber-Forensics & Training Alliance (NCFTA) is a non-profit corporation founded in 2002, focused on identifying, mitigating, and neutralizing cyber crime threats globally. The NCFTA operates by conducting real time information sharing and analysis with subject matter experts (SME) in the public, private, and academic sectors. Through these partnerships, the NCFTA proactively identifies cyber threats in order to help partners take preventive measures to mitigate those threats.

13. **National Institute of Standards and Technology (NIST), Applied Cybersecurity Division, National Initiative for Cybersecurity Education (NICE)**
    https://www.nist.gov/itl/applied-cybersecurity/nice

    NICE's "mission is to energize and promote a robust network and an ecosystem of cybersecurity education, training, and workforce development." NICE's strategic plan includes the following three goals:
    - Goal #1: Accelerate learning and skills development
    - Goal #2: Nurture a diverse learning community
    - Goal #3: Guide career development and workforce planning

14. **National Institute of Standards and Technology (NIST), Information Technology Laboratory**
    https://www.nist.gov/itl

    The Information Technology Laboratory (ITL), one of seven research laboratories within the National Institute of Standards and Technology (NIST), is a measurement and testing laboratory encompassing a wide range of areas of computer science, mathematics, statistics, and systems engineering.

15. **NUIX North America Inc. – The Black Report 2018: Decoding the Minds of Hackers**
    https://www.nuix.com/black-report/black-report-2018

    This report surveys professional hackers, penetration testers, and incident responds to help understand the security threat landscape.

16. **Russian Government–Cybersecurity**
    http://government.ru/en/
    http://government.ru/en/search/?q=cybersecurity&dt.till=11.05.2018&dt.
    since=7.05.2012&sort=rel&type=

    Topics include:
    - In Conversation with Dmitry Medvedev: Interview with five television channels
    - Sixth Open Innovations Moscow International Forum
    - Draft Guidelines on Russian Financial market's Development in 2016-2018

17. **SAFEKIDS**
    http://www.safekids.com/

    SafeKids.com is one of the oldest and most enduring sites for internet safety. Topics include: digital citizenship, online safety and civility.

18. **Talking with Kids About Being Online**
    https://www.whitehouse.gov/wp-content/uploads/2018/05/Talking-with-kids-about-being-online-_2018.pdf

    This guide from the Federal Trade Commission covers issues to raise kids about living their lives online
    - Talking to Your Kids
    - Communicating at Different Ages
    - Socializing Online
    - Using Mobile Devices
    - Making Computer Security a Habit
    - Protecting Your Child's Privacy

19. **US_CERT (United States Computer Emergency Readiness Team)**
    https://www.us-cert.gov/report-phishing
    https://www.antiphishing.org/about-APWG/APWG/

    US-CERT partners with the Anti-Phishing Working Group (APWG) to collect phishing e-mail messages and website locations to help people avoid becoming victims of phishing scams.
    APWG is the international coalition unifying the global response to cyber-crime across industry, government and law-enforcement sectors and NGO

communities. APWG's membership of more than 1800 institutions worldwide is as global as its outlook, with its directors, managers and research fellows advising: national governments, global governance bodies, hemispheric and global trade groups, multilateral treaty organizations, and the G8 High Technology Crime Subgroup.

- Avoiding social engineering and phishing attacks
- Protecting your privacy
- Understanding web site certificates
- Anti-phishing working group (APWG)
- Federal Trade Commission, identity theft
- Recognizing and avoiding e-mail scams

20. **USA.GOV**

https://www.usa.gov/common-scams-frauds

- Common scams and frauds
   - o Banking scams, IRS imposter scams, ticket scams, pyramid schemes
   - o Investment scams, Ponzi schemes, telephone scams, charity scams
   - o Lottery and sweepstakes scams, tax id theft, census related fraud
- Housing scams
   - o Avoid moving fraud, predatory loans, foreclosure scams, rental scams
- Identity theft
- Privacy
- Reporting scams frauds

Glossary

This glossary contains definitions of many terms used in this book, using language suited to the nontechnical reader. Terms used in definitions and defined elsewhere in the glossary are *italicized*.[1]

A

Alert—A *cybersecurity event* that undoubtedly indicates *malicious* behavior and generates an alarm on a detection system. The alarm indicates an *incident* is occurring and requires investigation and follow-up.

Authentication—The process of uniquely identifying oneself to a computer. Authentication is generally performed using a username and a *password*, although *strong authentication* or *multifactor authentication* may also be used.

Availability—One of the elements of the *cyber defense* triad of *confidentiality*, *integrity*, and *availability* (CIA). Availability refers to information technology services being available for use. An availability attack denies access to those services, usually through *denial of service* or *distributed denial of service* attacks.

B

Biometrics—A method of *strong authentication* that uses biological attributes such as fingerprints, iris patterns, or facial geometry to identify uniquely a person.

Botnet—A network of *compromised* computers that are all under an attacker's central control. It can be used to conduct *distributed denial-of-service* attacks or to obtain initial entry to a victim's *enterprise* through compromised computers.

Breach—The *compromise* of a system, networking resource, or data by an attacker who overcomes or defeats the established protection measures.

---

1 Material is adapted from Donaldson, S.E., Siegel, S. G., Williams, C.K., and Aslam, A. *Enterprise Cybersecurity: How to Build a Successful Cyberdefense Program Against Advanced Threats.* New York: Apress, 2015.

DOI 10.1515/9781501506505-017

C

CIA—The *cyber defense* triad of *confidentiality*, *integrity*, and *availability*. *Cyberattacks* involve compromising one or more of these properties of information technology systems, and *cyber defenses* involve protecting these properties.

Compromise—The act of taking control of a computer, *endpoint*, or *device* and modifying its configuration to suit the needs of the attacker. Frequently, compromise involves exploiting a *vulnerability* to install *malware* that gives the attacker some capability with regard to attacking the victim.

Confidentiality—One of the elements of the *cyber defense* triad of *confidentiality*, *integrity*, and *availability* (CIA). Confidentiality refers to the protection of data that should not be disclosed to people not authorized to have access to the data.

Credential—A parameter for *authentication* consisting of a user identity (e.g., *username*) and a proof of identity such as a *password* or *multifactor authentication token*.

Cryptography—*Cybersecurity* practice that includes processes for (1) generating numbers used to *encrypt* data so it can not be read by an attacker, (2) detecting changes made to data, and (3) verifying the original source of data.

Cyberattack—An attack conducted using computers and information systems to *compromise* the *confidentiality*, *integrity*, and/or *availability* of the target's information and information systems.

Cyber defense—The act of defending computers and information systems from *cyberattacks*.

Cybersecurity—The practice of protecting the *confidentiality*, *integrity*, and *availability* of information technology (IT) assets.

D

Denial of Service (DoS)—A *cyberattack* method that involves disabling IT systems either temporarily or permanently, thereby denying the *availability* to the intended users.

Device—A network-connected component that has computing capabilities but is not normally called a computer. Common devices are mobile phones, tablets, network-connected sensors, and computing appliances such as a printer.

Digital Signature—A *cryptographic* technique for protecting the *integrity* of data by calculating a *hash* of the data and then cryptographically processing the hash through an industry certified organization. This technique makes it possible to prove the authenticity of the data, detect unauthorized changes, and achieve nonrepudiation.

Distributed Denial of Service (DDoS)—A *denial of service* attack that uses a distributed network—usually a *botnet*—to overload IT systems with a massive surge of network traffic that the infrastructure is unable to handle.

E

Encryption—A *cryptographic* technique for protecting data so it can only be read by holders of the legitimate *key*.

Endpoint—Any type of computing system, including servers, personal computers, appliances, mobile *devices* such as smartphones, or other network-connected devices. Endpoints are subject to security policies and capabilities intended to prevent their *compromise.*

Enterprise—An organization that uses computers or computer networks for personal, business, and country (also known as, nation-state) purposes. An enterprise has authority over those computers and computer networks. An enterprise may range from an individual's personal computer and network up to a corporate or governmental entity with thousands or hundreds of thousands of computers connected to networks spanning the globe.

Escalate Privileges—In a *cyberattack*, attackers obtain additional privileges in the *enterprise*. For example, going from regular user to *systems administrator* status on a personal computer or file server or escalating from computer administrator to network administrator status on an enterprise network.

Event—An incidence of behavior that is documented and may be an indication of *malicious* behavior. *Incidents* are generated when one or more events together constitute an *indicator of compromise* and warrant investigation.

F, G

Firewall—A hardware or software security capability that connects to a network and applies a security *policy* to determine what network traffic is allowed to pass and what network traffic is blocked. It can also *alert* on certain types of network traffic that might indicate an attack.

Forensics—The science of investigating *compromised* computer systems to understand attacker *tools, techniques,* and *procedures,* and also to determine *indicators* *of compromise.* Forensic investigation involves analyzing logs, files, and sometimes program code to understand *attacker* activities and methods.

H

Hash—A fixed-length *cryptographic* code calculated from a document or data field such that any change to the document or data field results in the hash changing as well. The algorithm is one-way so knowledge of the hash does not lead to the original document or data being revealed. This capability is used to protect the *integrity* of documents from modification, as well as for *authentication* so *passwords* do not need to be stored unencrypted.

I, J

Incident—A *cybersecurity* activity initiated by one or more *events* or *alerts* that indicate *malicious* behavior and warrant investigation. Incidents are investigated using *security information and event management* systems, and computer *forensics.*

Incident Response—The practice of investigating, containing, remediating, resolving, and documenting *cybersecurity incidents*, using *indicators of compromise* and performing *forensics* on *compromised* systems.

Indicator of Compromise (IOC)—An indicator that can be used to identify *attacker malicious* activity in the *enterprise*. Indicators are usually accounts, computers, network addresses, or communications patterns that are identified using *forensics* and then used to generate additional *alerts* to identify *cyberattack* activity wherever it is occurring.

Integrity—One of the elements of the *cyber defense* triad of *confidentiality, integrity,* and *availability* (CIA). Integrity refers to having confidence that data is not changed by unauthorized people from when it is input into a computer system until it is later retrieved from the computer system. Integrity is particularly important for financial records, medical records, and transactions, but it can also apply to system configurations and other aspects of IT systems. Integrity attacks involve changing data or configurations through unauthorized means.

K

Keys—In *cryptography*, digital strings that are used to *encrypt*, decrypt (i.e., convert encrypted information back into plain language) and *digitally sign* data.

L

Lateral Movement—In a *cyberattack*, moving from one computer to another where both machines are at equivalent levels of *privilege*, or using credentials at a single privilege level. Lateral movement is in contrast with *escalating privileges*, where attackers obtain additional privileges within the victim environment.

M

Malicious—Adjective applied to behavior, network traffic, or software intended to *compromise* the *confidentiality*, *integrity*, or *availability* of *enterprise* data and IT systems.

Malware—*Malicious* software. Malware is generally characterized by one or more of the following properties: (1) it attempts to stay hidden or to persist on the victim computer after attempts to remove it, (2) it attempts to propagate from one victim computer to another, (3) it collects data from the victim computer and sends it to another computer, (4) it collects user *credentials* for resources and/or websites, or (5) it *monitors* user behavior without the user's knowledge or consent.

Monitoring—Collecting and storing data, *events*, or *alerts* so they can be consolidated into one location for correlation and analysis in a *security information and event management* system. Monitoring can be for operational purposes—to help ensure systems are performing properly—or for *cybersecurity* purposes to detect *incidents*.

Multifactor Authentication—*Authentication* that relies on multiple factors of identity, usually something the user knows such as a *password*, plus something the user has such as a *token* or mobile *device*, or possibly a *biometric* such as a fingerprint (also known as, *two-factor authentication* or *strong authentication*).

N

Nonrepudiation—Electronic proof of identity. Generally, nonrepudiation is performed *cryptographically* by *digitally signing* a unique piece of data using a *key* that is only help by the party, thus providing the party's identity online.

O

One-Time Password—A *password* that is only used for a single *authentication* attempt.

P, Q

Password—A string of characters known only to the user and used to *authenticate*, proving the user's identity to a computer system.

Patch—A software or configuration update that addresses a performance or security issue that is distributed and installed after a system is in production.

Policy—In cybersecurity, a management statement of behavior to be performed within the *enterprise*.

Privilege—Permission for access to an *enterprise* computer resource. *Attackers* frequently seek to obtain administrative privileges to computer system and data. With administrator privileges, attackers can access and modify data at will.

R

Risk—In *cybersecurity*, the chance or likelihood that an attacker or *threat* interferes with the *confidentiality*, *integrity*, or *availability* of data or IT services. Normally, risk is analyzed based upon threats exploiting present *vulnerabilities* and causing an impact to the data or IT services.

S

Security Information and Event Management (SIEM)—Technology for collecting and matching *cybersecurity events* and *alerts*, and investigating and tracking *incidents* arising from them.

Strong Authentication—*Authentication* that relies on multiple factors of identity, usually something the user knows such as a *password*, plus something the user has such as a *token* or mobile *device*, or possibly a *biometric* such as a fingerprint (also known as, *multifactor authentication* or *two-factor authentication*).

Systems Administrator—An individual who administers a computer system. Generally, the systems administrator has *privileges* to be able to modify all data and software on the system, including applications and the operating systems. Many attacks involve obtaining systems administrator privileges.

T

Threat—An entity—someone or something—that can exploit an associated *vulnerability*.

Token—In *authentication*, a physical device used for *multifactor authentication*. Users prove they are in possession of the token usually by generating a *cryptographic* code from *keys* stored within it. Users then enter the *cryptographic* code into the computer by typing it or through some type of electronic connection.

Tools, Techniques, and Procedures (TTPs)—In computer *forensics*, identification of how *attackers* are operating: (1) the applications and other tools they are using, (2) the techniques with which they are using those tools, and (3) the procedures they are following to perform those techniques. *TTPs* are important *indicators of compromise* used to track down attackers and repel them in an *incident response*.

Two-Factor Authentication—*Authentication* that relies on multiple factors of identify, usually something the user knows such as a *password*, plus something the user has such as a *token* or mobile *device*, or possibly a *biometric* such as a fingerprint (also known as, *multifactor authentication* or *strong authentication*).

U

Username—A unique identification such as a login name associated with a specific user who is allowed access to *endpoints* such as personal computers, mobile *devices*, or computer networks.

V, W, X, Y

Virtual Private Network (VPN)—A network security technology that involves creating an *encrypted* tunnel from one host computer to another over an untrusted network. This encrypted tunnel is used to connect the networks at both ends so they are "virtually" connected and "private" from the network in between.

Virus—A form of *malware* that attaches itself to other pieces of software in order to propagate and run. A virus can be embedded into an application or computer operating system, but it is unable to run on its own. It usually includes the ability to replicate itself, and it may also have a payload to perform some type of destructive or *malicious* behavior.

Vulnerability—A flaw that allows a system to be exploited or *compromised* for *malicious* purposes. Vulnerabilities may be flaws in software code, system configurations, or security architectures. Some vulnerabilities are remediated through *patches*, while others may require significant system redesign or technology replacement.

Z

Zero-Day-Exploit—A cyberattack that targets a *vulnerability* not publicly known or for which a *patch* is not yet available.

Index

DOI 10.1515/9781501506505-018

Made in the USA
Coppell, TX
16 January 2022

71717351R00116